Catching up with
Computers

Catching up with
Computers
The over-50s' survival guide

Moira Stephen

An imprint of Pearson Education

**London New York Toronto Sydney Tokyo Singapore
Madrid Mexico City Munich Paris**

PEARSON EDUCATION LIMITED

Head Office:
Edinburgh Gate
Harlow CM20 2JE
Tel: +44 (0)1279 623623
Fax: +44 (0)1279 431059

London Office:
128 Long Acre
London WC2E 9AN
Tel: +44 (0)20 7447 2000
Fax: +44 (0)20 7240 5771
Website: *www.it-minds.com*

First published in Great Britain in 2001

© Pearson Education Limited 2001

ISBN 0-130-90823-1

British Library Cataloguing-in-Publication Data
A catalogue record for this book is available from the British Library.

10 9 8 7 6 5 4 3 2 1

Trademark/Registered Trademarks
Computer hardware and software brand names mentioned in this book are
protected by their respective trademarks and are acknowledged.

♛ Typeset by Elle & P.K. McBride, Southampton
Printed in Great Britain by Biddles Ltd, Guildford.

The publishers' policy is to use paper manufactured from sustainable forests.

Contents

POWER POINT →

Conventions in this book

Menu instructions are separated by a ▶. The instruction:

Click **View** ▶ **Toolbars** ▶ **Print Preview**

means open the **View** menu, click on **Toolbars** then click **Print Preview**.

Key presses are enclosed within square brackets, e.g. **[Ctrl]** means press the Ctrl key.

The instruction **[Ctrl]-[B]** means hold down the Ctrl key and at the same time press B.

1
Getting Started

IN THIS CHAPTER:

- History lesson
- Living with computers
- Overview of a PC
- Software
- Networks

We start with a brief history, followed by a discussion on computers in everyday life. Then comes the 'computer speak'. Many of the terms and jargon that you are likely to hear – from friends, salesmen, on the TV and in newspapers – will be discussed so that the gobbledegook makes sense! You won't be able to use your computer by the end of this chapter, but you should have a better understanding of the environment you are about to experience.

History lesson

19th century

Some of the theories and ideas that would eventually come together to help make up the modern computer were conceived back in the 19th century.

1830s – Babbage's Analytical Engine conceived

In the 1830s Charles Babbage (an English inventor) came up with a number of mechanical calculating machines. His most famous was called the *Analytical Engine*. Although never actually built, the intention was that it would perform some of the tasks a digital computer performs today, e.g. store instructions, perform calculations and have a permanent memory (punched cards would have been used). Had it been built it would have been huge – covering an area about the size of a football pitch!

During the 19th century, an English mathematician called George Boole devised a system of mathematics called Boolean algebra. The system used the digits 0 and 1 only. This system has become particularly useful in digital computers as they use millions of tiny switches that could be on or off – represented by a 0 or 1. The on-off switches became known as bits, for *b*inary dig*its*. The bit is the fundamental building block of the modern computer.

Analogue computers began to be built towards the end of the 19th century.

1889 – Hollerith's calculating machine

Towards the end of the century Herman Hollerith (an American inventor) patented a calculating machine. It used punched cards and in 1890 it was used to compute census data.

20th century

1924 – IBM founded

In the first quarter of the century Hollerith's Tabulating Machine Company experienced several mergers. It was finally absorbed into a company which adopted the name International Business Machines Corporation (IBM).

World War II provided a huge stimulus to computer development.

World War II – great stimulus to computer development

Howard Aiken (an American) led the development of a computer known as the Mark 1. It used 3304 on-off switches to create ballistic tables used by the naval artillery.

The British developed a computer using valves instead of switches and used it to decode German messages.

Shortly after the war the Americans built the ENIAC – the most sophisticated computer of its time. It was big, taking up about 450 sq m (4500 sq ft) and contained 17,468 valves. Although impressive at the time, it had less capacity than a modern laptop computer.

In 1947 Bell Laboratories in the US invented the transistor – which was much smaller, quicker and cheaper than valves.

1947 – transistor invented

A few years later the microchip and microprocessor were invented. These developments allowed information to be stored and manipulated in a small space.

Index cards were used for many data-sorting operations during the 1960s.

A company called Micro Instrumentation Telemetry Systems (MITS), in Albuquerque, New Mexico, released the Altair 8800 in 1974. This was a personal computer kit (unassembled!) costing less than $400. It had no keyboard, only a panel of switches with which to enter information. Its capacity was less than one per cent of that of a handheld computer in 1991.

1974 – first PC, the Altair 8800 released

In 1975 co-founders of the Microsoft Corporation, William H. Gates III (Bill Gates) and Paul Allen collaborated on the first version of the BASIC programming language for the MITS Altair. The Microsoft Corporation was founded in Albuquerque, New Mexico in 1975.

1975 – Microsoft Corporation founded

Gates and Allen moved Microsoft to a suburb of their home town of Seattle, Washington in 1979.

In the 1980s, computers became progressively smaller, better, and cheaper. As the hardware became more powerful, software became more sophisticated. It pushed the limits of the hardware, encouraging the building of new machines with bigger drives, faster processors, and larger memories.

1981 – MS-DOS
released

Microsoft took its first step in diversifying beyond the programming languages market when it released MS-DOS, the operating system for the original IBM personal computer (PC) in 1981. Microsoft went on to convince other PC manufacturers to license MS-DOS, which made it the de facto software standard for PCs.

In 1969, ARPAnet, a long-distance computer network devised by the US Government's Advanced Research Projects Agency saw the first faltering steps of what is now the Internet. From an initial network of four computers in 1969, another 200 computers in military and research establishments throughout the USA were linked together using this network during the 1970s. By the mid-1980s several academic networks had also been set up. These combined with the ARPAnet to form the Internet.

The **Internet**
emerged in the
mid-1980s

Another significant area of development for Microsoft was its move into the application software business.

By 1984 Microsoft was one of the few established software companies to develop application software for the original Apple Macintosh. When Microsoft later released Windows, its graphical operating system for IBM compatible personal computers, its experience on graphical applications for the Macintosh led to success with Windows applications such as the Microsoft Excel spreadsheet and the Microsoft Word word processing programs. Today, these applications are designed to behave similarly on Windows and the Macintosh.

1984 – Microsoft
developed
application
software for the
Apple Mac

1991 – IBM and
Microsoft go their
separate ways

1991 saw the end of a decade of collaboration between Microsoft and IBM when they went their separate ways on the next generation of operating systems for personal computers. IBM chose to pursue a former joint venture with Microsoft on the OS/2 operating system, while Microsoft chose to further evolve its Windows operating system.

By 1992 the computer industry was the fastest-growing industry in the world. Competition between major hardware and software companies was fierce and there were many casualties.

The 1990s saw the rapid development of the Windows operating system – Windows 3.1, Windows 95, 98 and 98SE,

Windows NT, Windows 2000 and Windows Me were all re-leased, each version bigger and more powerful than the previous. The Microsoft Office Suite went from release 4.2, to Office 95, Office 97 then Office 2000. Lotus and WordPerfect also developed and delivered more powerful applications.

In **1992**, Microsoft delivered Windows 3.1.

The Internet became an exciting, fast-growing area with computer users getting hooked up at a phenomenal rate.

By the end of the 20th century, Microsoft had certainly cornered the lion's share of the PC software market with its Windows operating system, desktop applications and Internet browser software. Allegations of 'dirty deeds' by the Microsoft Corporation as it exploited its dominant position to squeeze out competitors resulted in legal proceedings.

21st century

Microsoft starts the 21st century in the courts!

Computers are everywhere! They guide aircraft, control traffic, process words and numbers, store medical and dental records, and keep track of appointments – not to mention store your photographs and play your videos and music! You can use them to book your holidays, buy your wine, do your banking or research your favourite hobby.

They have become the heart of modern business, research, and, indeed, everyday life.

Living with computers

Bill Gates (co-founder of Microsoft Corporation) had a vision of there being a computer on every desk and in every home – a vision that is rapidly becoming a reality in the developed world.

We live in an *Information Society*. Information – we work with it, play with it, and keep generating more of it!

The term *Information Superhighway* is used to describe a situation where information of any kind, anywhere in the world, would be available to anyone who had access to a PC linked to the Internet.

Information Society – where a high proportion of people work with information and where people have access to a vast amount of information via the Internet

At home

Many homes have computers and this number is on the increase. Most home computers are *multimedia* systems that can be used for work and play.

Multimedia system – a computer that can run games and application software, play music and videos, access the Internet, etc.

A computer at home has many uses:

- Word processing software allows people to create letters, reports, invitations, lists, etc. Spreadsheet software can help you manage your home accounts and budgets.
- Homework and research – school pupils and students can find a home PC very useful. Encyclopedias are available on CD and the Internet gives access to information on any subject you care to mention.
- Home banking – Internet access on a home PC can give you home banking (if your bank provides the facility).
- Computer games are also popular on home PCs (games can also be played via the Internet).

Home shopping – you can buy almost anything over the Internet from a tin of beans to a house

- Home shopping is on the increase – many high street shops have Web sites and specialist Internet retailers, e.g. Amazon.com, have emerged.

SoHo = small office/home office, a term associated with home working

- Home working – the number of people working from home has increased as many jobs that traditionally had to be done in the office can be carried out successfully on a PC at home. The benefits of home working are that it is flexible (you don't need to stick to the 9–5 routine), and you don't need to join the commuter trail to and from the office each day. However, some home workers feel isolated as they miss the social interaction of a central office.
- E-mail can be used to communicate quickly (and cheaply) with friends and family anywhere in the world.

On a day-to-day basis, the following areas of your life are influenced by computers:

- Bills – gas, electricity, water, telephone, etc. are all computerised.

ATMs – you've probably used this computer system if no other!

- Money – Automatic Teller Machines (ATMs), or debit and credit cards use computers to record transactions.
- Medical records – many doctors and dentists keep patient records on computer.

- Supermarkets – barcode readers identify the product bought and the price is located on computer, the stock records are adjusted to reflect the sale.
- Library books – many libraries use electronic tagging to facilitate computerised records of when books are issued and when they should be returned.
- Smart cards – cards with a microchip that contains a considerable amount of information about the holder could be used as combined debit/credit cards, identity cards, driving licence, record of emergency medical details, etc. Although still relatively new, their use will most likely increase in the future.

At work

Typical office applications software includes:

- *Word processing* for letters, reports, minutes, memos, etc.;
- *Spreadsheet* for budgets, sales figures and anything involving calculations;
- *Database* for customer records, supplier information, product information, personnel records;
- *Presentation* for meetings, lectures, conferences;
- *Information management*, e.g. electronic diaries and organisers;
- *Accounts* to keep tabs on purchases and sales and prepare invoices and statements;
- *Desktop publishing* for newsletters, leaflets, posters, etc.

Typical business applications may include word processing, spreadsheets, database, presentation, desktop publishing, accounts and information management

Specialised businesses may use applications specific to their area of work, e.g. graphic design packages or photographic image manipulation packages.

In industry, processors and computers are used to control production lines, the manufacturing process and for stock control. *Computer Assisted Design* and *Computer Assisted Manufacturing (CAD/CAM)* is used to design components, and the design information is then used to control the machine that manufactures the components

In the public sector, Government agencies use computers to store NHS records, housing information, social security records, criminal records, etc.

Electronic Data Interchange (EDI)

EDI allows many operations to be fully automated – stock control, reordering, invoicing, despatch and payment

This refers to a situation where all communications in a business transaction are done electronically. An example would be the use of computers in a retail environment. As items are purchased by the customer, details of the item are entered into the computer via the barcode reader at the checkout. This information automatically updates the stock records. When the stock levels reach the reorder level, an order would be raised and sent to the supplier electronically (using an EDI facility) and payment could be authorised at the same time. The supplier's computer would respond electronically to the order, arrange despatch of the goods and prepare and send the invoice.

E-commerce

E-commerce is a rapidly expanding business area

The Internet has facilitated the expansion of e-commerce. Companies can advertise their products on their own Web sites on the Internet, take orders and accept payment via secure credit card transfer.

Video conferencing

Video conferencing allows business meetings to take place between people in different locations (towns or even countries) without them having to spend time and money travelling

Business people worldwide can have face-to-face meetings using video conferencing. Video cameras are linked via computers and the Internet so that people can see who they are talking to without leaving their office. A lot of time and money can be saved by holding meetings this way. People do not need to spend time and money travelling, or pay expensive hotel bills.

Okay, so there you have it! A potted history of computers, and a quick look at the many areas of our lives where computers are in evidence. Whether at home or at work it's very difficult to escape from them – and let's face it, where would we be without them!

Different types of computer

There are several different kinds of computer. The one that you are probably most familiar with is the Personal Computer – the PC. A brief description of the different types of computer you are likely to hear mentioned follows.

Personal Computers (PC)

The type of computer that you are most likely to use is the PC. Originally the PC was developed and marketed by IBM. Launched in 1981 it became a great success, so much so that other companies copied it and marketed their own PC 'clone' as an IBM compatible PC. A modern PC consists of a monitor (also called a visual display unit or VDU), keyboard, mouse and a box containing the electronics, hard disk, memory, diskette drive, etc. The box may be under the monitor (in a desktop model), or it may be standing beside it or on the floor under it (if the box is a tower model).

PC – a desktop computer, designed for individual use

Hard disk – a storage device for data. The disk is housed in a disk drive

Laptops

As people began to rely more on their PC for business and personal use, the demand for a portable PC grew. This led to the development of *laptops* – smaller PCs powered by batteries, that could be carried about in a briefcase. As the PCs were battery powered they would only work for a few hours before they had to be recharged – which meant you might need to take the charger with you (and perhaps a spare battery). Portable printers were designed so that you could print out your work while you were out and about, and, if you wanted to send/receive data and faxes, a cellular phone (connected to your laptop using an interface card and cable) could be used. A large (pretty large) briefcase would be needed to carry all this hardware – useful, but perhaps a less 'portable' solution than it first appears.

Laptop – a small(ish), portable PC

Palmtops/Hand-held devices

These PCs are small enough to be held in the palm of your hand. They use scaled-down versions of desktop software, e.g. Windows CE.

The market leader in palmtop computers over the past few years has been the PSION range – strictly speaking not a PC at all as it uses a different operating system and software.

Network computers

Network – computers connected together so that they can share resources and transfer information

You can use your PC as a stand-alone computer, or link it to other computers to form a network. PCs can be networked in a simple *peer-to-peer* setup that allows peripherals, e.g. printers, scanners to be shared. A user can also access files on another user's hard drive in this type of network.

Folders can be created on disks to help you manage your disk space efficiently

Alternatively, PCs can be networked through a central computer (called a *server* or *file server*) where they can share disks and *folders*. Each user is allocated a specific area of hard disk on the file server for their own data files. The file server also stores main application software that can be run over the whole network, e.g. e-mail, anti-virus, etc. Backup procedures are simplified for the user in this setup as all files on the file server can be backed up at the same time (often at night, when most people have stopped work and gone home) rather than each user having to back up the files from their own PC.

File servers are intended for business rather than personal use and they are more expensive than standard PCs.

Supercomputers, mainframes and minicomputers

The most powerful mainframes are called supercomputers. They are used heavily in both pure and applied research by scientists, large businesses and the military, to perform extremely complex and time-consuming computations.

Mainframes and minicomputers are much bigger than PCs (although PCs and terminals may be connected to them via a network).

Mainframes are large file servers that can store and process the data for a whole organisation. Banks, insurance companies and retail stores, e.g. Boots, will often use mainframes.

Smaller organisations may be able to get by using a mini-computer. Some minicomputers can be networked into a 'cluster' to take on tasks that a mainframe might perform.

Data input terminals

These *look* like computers, but are actually input devices for the computer proper. You may have seen a data input terminal in action at the checkout of your local store where the barcode reader scans the item purchased and enters the data into the central computer. The central computer will process the data that has been entered via the data input terminal. The central computer may deal with stock control and re-ordering of goods as necessary. You will also encounter data input terminals at your bank and in the travel agent when you go to book your holiday – the terminal can be used to display information and enter details of bookings.

Some data input terminals have limited processing capabilities, and these terminals are called *intelligent* terminals. Terminals with no processing capabilities are called *dumb* terminals.

Backup – a procedure where files are copied for security reasons

Supercomputer – a very powerful mainframe

Overview of a PC

Whatever you use your PC for – word processing, e-mail, accounts, desktop publishing, etc. – the main actions are:

- Input – text, data and instructions are input to the computer, usually through the keyboard or by using the mouse;
- Process – the computer processes the text and data according to instructions;
- Store – your data can be saved to a storage device, e.g. disk;
- Output – the results are output, e.g. to the VDU or printer.

This book discusses computing in the context of PCs/ laptops from this point forward

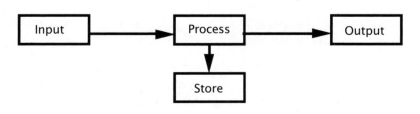

These actions are performed using the various devices that make up your computer. Typically, a computer consists of:

Peripheral – any piece of equipment attatched to a PC, e.g. printer, speakers, rather than built into it

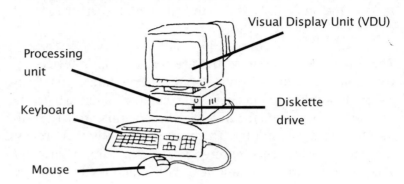

Visual Display Unit (VDU)

Processing unit

Keyboard

Diskette drive

Mouse

Most computers are linked to a printer, and your computer may have other devices, e.g. speakers, scanner, digital camera, CD, DVD, etc.

Hardware – the physical parts of your computer and peripherals are all hardware

Hardware

The keyboard, mouse, trackball, visual display unit (VDU) or monitor, printer, storage devices (hard drive, diskette), speakers, central processing unit, electronic components, boards, memory components, etc. are all items of hardware.

Input device – any device that enables you to enter data or give instructions to your computer

Input devices

Keyboard – Used to type information (both instructions and data) into your computer.

Mouse – A mouse allows data input by selecting options (rather than typing in) – you click on the option required.

Trackball and **touchpad** – These are often found on laptops in place of a mouse. A trackball is like an upside-down mouse, and you use your fingertips to move the ball (which has the effect of moving the mouse pointer on the screen). A touchpad senses a fingertip being drawn across it and moves the mouse pointer on the screen accordingly.

Scanner – These are used to convert printed material into a digitised form that can be imported into an application package. The scanner will take a 'picture' of the printed material, and the picture can then be stored or viewed on your PC. If you wish to scan in text and then manipulate the text using a word processing application, the scanner will need Optical Character Recognition (OCR) software. This software will convert the printed image into a form that can be used in a word processing application.

Graphics tablet – This is a touch-sensitive pad that has a stylus attached to it. The stylus can be used to write or draw freehand onto the pad, and the data is converted into a digitised form that can be used in your computer.

Digital camera – Photographic images are stored in a digital format in the camera. The images can then be downloaded into your PC, and edited/printed and stored as required.

Voice recognition – A microphone is attached to a PC that has appropriate voice recognition software on it. When you speak into the microphone the speech is converted into text. The text can then be stored, edited and printed as required. This method of input could be very useful for visually or physically impaired PC users.

Joystick – Used to play games.

Output devices

Visual Display Unit (VDU) – Information that has been entered into the computer can be viewed on the VDU (also called a *monitor*).

Output device – any device that allows what is on your PC to be seen or heard

The size of a VDU varies. The measurement quoted is for the *diagonal* measurement of the screen itself. Most PCs come with a 14" or 15" VDU as standard, with 17" monitors becoming standard on some systems (the more expensive ones). Prices are coming down and 17", 19" and 21" VDUs are becoming more affordable.

The *resolution* of a VDU refers to the number of pixels on the screen. Generally speaking, the more pixels the better the picture. A resolution of 640 × 480 means that there are 640 pixels across the screen, 480 down the screen. A resolution of 800 × 600 is also common.

Pixels – dots of light on the screen

The display quality is also affected by the *refresh rate* (or *scan rate*). This is the frequency at which the dots of light flash on the screen. Typically, the refresh rate is 60 times per second.

Printer – Printers are used to produce hard copy (printouts) of the data in your computer – text, graphs, pictures, etc. There are different types of printers, each with their own advantages and disadvantages. Inkjet printers are good for home use (or where low-volume printing is required) – they are fairly cheap to buy, but the ink cartridge is quite expensive. Laser printers are good for business use where high-quality high-volume printing is required. These printers are quite expensive to buy, but the running costs are less when high volume is required. You may also come across a dot matrix printer – an older, noisier type of printer. Cheap, but not as popular as they once were.

Plotters – A specialised type of printer used in design environments for things like technical drawings or architectural plans. They can print out large, complex hard copies. The

Summary of printer types				
	How it works	Price	Running cost	Other info
Dot matrix	Small pins are grouped together to form letters; the pins hit a ribbon giving the letter shape on the paper	Cheap: < £100	Cheap: ribbons last a long time	Poor quality output. Noisy. Not used much except perhaps to print invoices, etc. Reasonably quick.
Ink jet	Uses an ink cartridge, giving a very fine spray to form the letters, etc.	Fairly cheap: £80–£250	Cartridges relatively expensive - about £25	Colour models give impressive results. Good for low-volume, home use. Speed 3–12 ppm (pages per minute).
Laser	'Burn' the words onto the paper	Expensive: £400 – £3000	Low running costs per page printed	Quicker than other types – up to 24 ppm. Good investment for long-term heavy use.

computer software controls a type of pen that moves in two dimensions over paper.

Speakers – These tend to come as standard on a *multimedia* PC, which is the type often purchased for home use. They work in exactly the same way as speakers attached to your stereo equipment. Speakers on a PC may be self-powered, with a small amplifier built in. They usually require a soundcard to be fitted inside the computer and the speakers are then connected to this card.

Speech synthesiser – The software in this device translates written text into audible speech. It has specialist uses, e.g. to help people with impaired vision or those with physical disabilities.

Central Processing Unit (CPU)

The CPU is often referred to as the *brain* of the computer. It performs the core processing, logic control and calculation work on the information which is either input by the operator or specified by the software. It controls the information flow between the disks and main memory.

A **CPU** constructed on a single chip is called a microprocessor

The *clock speed* of the CPU is the speed at which it can process information. The clock speed is measured in megahertz (MHz). A clock speed of 600 MHz means that the processor can operate at 600 million cycles per second.

Mega = million
Hertz = cycles per second

The clock speed of a computer is *one* of the factors that can influence its performance. Generally speaking, the higher the clock speed the more expensive the computer.

Intel (with its Pentium range) and AMD (with its K series) are the main producers and suppliers of microprocessors.

Processing unit – The processing unit (either a desktop or tower metal or plastic box) contains:

Electronics e.g. the Central Processing Unit (CPU) and other microchips, e.g. memory chips (see page 16 – 17).

Hard disk drive – a storage device. Used for storing programs and data (see page 17).

Floppy disk drive – allows a diskette to be used for storage. Facilitates the easy transfer of data (and programs) from one computer to another.

CD-ROM drive – reads information from a standard CD (similar to a music CD). The CD may contain music or applications software or data. Most applications are issued on CD. New computers may have a DVD drive instead of a CD drive (see page 18).

Modem – allows the PC to connect to the telephone system and use e-mail and the Internet (some PCs have an *external* modem rather than an *internal* one).

Storage – The unit of measurement used to describe disk capacity and memory size on computers are bits, bytes, kilobytes, megabytes and gigabytes. As storage capacity is constantly increasing, the measurements most often used are megabytes (Mb) and gigabytes (Gb).

Unit of measurement	
1 bit	The amount of memory space needed to hold either 1 or 0
1 byte	Equal to 8 bits. Every letter or number is made up of 8 bits (one byte), so each takes up one byte of storage space
1 kilobyte (Kb)	1024 bytes. Double-density diskettes have a capacity of 720Kb
1 megabyte (Mb)	1024 kilobytes. Memory size is usually quoted in Mb – about 1 million bytes. Typically a PC will have between 16 and 64Mb of memory (although more can be added if required). High-density diskettes have a capacity of 1.44Mb
1 gigabyte (Gb)	1024 megabytes (about 1 billion bytes). Hard disk sizes are usually quoted in Gb; on new PCs the hard disk is typically about 10Gb

Types of memory

Random Access Memory (RAM)

RAM – when the computer is switched off anything in RAM is lost

Often referred to as *main memory*. The programs and data you are working on are stored in RAM. The CPU controls the flow of programs and data to and from RAM. Data that has been stored on disk is transferred into RAM when you open the file to work on it.

PCs will typically have between 16Mb and 64Mb of RAM. Many new applications will not run satisfactorily on less than 16Mb. It is normally possible to add more RAM if you wish.

Read Only Memory (ROM)

Similar to RAM, but its contents are not lost when the computer is switched off. The CPU can read the contents of ROM, but can't add to it. ROM is also available on CDs and DVDs.

ROM – Read Only Memory, you can read from it but can't write to it

Disks

Hard disks

A PC will usually be sold with a hard disk drive (HDD) built into it. However, you can buy additional HDDs to increase your storage space – you can get HDDs to fit inside your PC (an internal drive), or ones that plug into your PC but sit outside the unit as a *peripheral* (an external drive). External drives are more expensive than internal ones, and the cost of a drive rises with its capacity. The capacity of HDDs is increasing but typically they store from 6Gb to 30Gb. In general, larger capacity HDDs have faster access times than smaller ones.

Your HDD will hold your application software (word processing, spreadsheets, etc.) and your data.

– the time taken for the unit to search for, identify and process data saved on the disk, measured in milliseconds (msec) for a HDD

Floppy disk

A floppy disk drive uses floppy disks (diskettes). These normally store less information than HDDs. Other than capacity, the main difference between them is that diskettes are portable (unlike HDDs, which are inside or plugged into your PC). Diskettes are often used for backup copies of data files, in case the originals get damaged. They are the cheapest type of storage media, but are becoming less popular as higher capacity options become available at a reasonable price.

Iomega Zip drives

These drives have become increasingly popular in recent years. They combine the portability of a diskette with a higher capacity disk (originally 100Mb, with 250Mb disks now on the market). The Zip drives use special Zip disks, which look similar to, but a little bigger than, diskettes. Zip drives can be fitted internally or externally.

Compact discs (CD-ROM)

CDs have been used on PCs for several years. CD-ROMS can store up to 650Mb and are ideally suited for information that doesn't need to be updated often, e.g. application packages, encyclopedias like Encarta, clipart, etc. In addition to storage capacity, increased speed of access is another benefit of CDs.

CDs (like all other areas of IT) are continually developing. Recent developments have resulted in CDs that you can write to (store data on), in the same way as a HDD. There are two types of CDs that you can write to – CD-R (Recordable) and CD-RW (ReWriteable). With a CD-R you can use the disk to record information once only – once you've recorded something on it you can't re-record. With a CD-RW you can record, and re-record, as often as you want – the disks are reusable.

DVDs (Digital Versatile Discs)

Disks, CDs, DVDs etc. = Secondary Storage

Although relatively new, these disks are beginning to supersede CDs. They have storage capacities of 4–5 Gb. You can store audio, video or computer data on a DVD. CD-ROMs can be used in a DVD drive, but a DVD disk will not operate in a CD drive. DVD-R (recordable) is also available.

To summarise the advances in CD technology from the mid-1990s, we have had:

CD (ROM) ⟶ CD-R ⟶ CD-RW ⟶ DVD ⟶ DVD-R

PC performance

You can judge a computer's performance in a number of ways – perhaps by the amount of time it takes to open an application or file, or the amount of time it takes to display a graphic on the screen. Things that may affect performance are:
*   The clock speed of the CPU
*   The amount of RAM
*   The size of the HDD
*   The access speed of the HDD

• The access speed of any peripheral device that the computer gets information from, e.g. modem, external drives.

For a PC to operate at its optimum level, the capability of components has to be balanced. There is little point having 128Mb of RAM and a 30Gb HDD on a computer with a 133MHz chip – the processor speed would not allow the optimum performance of the memory or HDD.

Software

There are two types of software that you should be aware of: *operating system* and *application package* software.

Software – the 'programs' that make your computer work

Operating system

The OS is essential to the efficient running of the PC. It controls which operations within the computer are carried out and in what order they are done. It ensures that when you press a key on your keyboard, the instruction is translated into something the computer can work with.

OS = Operating System

When a computer is switched on it is said to *boot-up.* During the boot-up process it carries out a Power On Self Test (POST) to check that the hardware components are present and working properly and to check that the CPU and memory are functioning correctly. The next thing that the computer does when it boots up is to locate and load the OS (or part of the OS). The OS is usually stored on the hard disk, e.g in your Windows *folder.* The OS is loaded into RAM at this stage.

POST = Power On Self Test

Folders are covered in Chapter 3

The OS that you will become familiar with when working through this book is Microsoft Windows – you may be using Windows 95, 98, Me, NT, or Windows 2000.

Windows has a Graphical User Interface (GUI) - it uses pictures (icons) to show the facilities available on the PC rather than words. You can select a feature by pointing to it with the mouse and then clicking on the feature you want to choose. Using a GUI as the front end to an OS makes it much easier for a user to tell the system what to do. Apple Macs also have a GUI.

Application packages

Programs like word processing, spreadsheet, database, etc. are called application packages. These are separate from the OS, but they must be compatible with it. If you read the information on the box of an application package in a PC store, it will tell you what OS it is compatible with.

There are many popular application packages that can be used at work or in the home, e.g. word processing, spreadsheet, database, presentation, desktop publishing (DTP), games etc.

Many application packages are sold as a *suite*, e.g. Microsoft Office or Microsoft Works. The suites contain a set of packages, e.g. word processing, spreadsheet, presentation, database, desktop publishing. Both Works and Office are popular suites found in the home and in all types of businesses. The applications in Office are more powerful and sophisticated than those in Works making it more suited to business use. Other suppliers also produce suites, e.g. Lotus Smart Suite.

Networks

Two or more computers connected together form a *network*. A network may consist a couple of computers in the same office sharing a printer and files or thousands of computers connected across the globe.

LAN

LAN = Local Area Network

A LAN is made up of computers connected by cables, in the same room or building. The computers are in close proximity (local) to each other. Benefits of linking PCs together into a LAN are that several PCs can share the same peripherals, e.g. printer, scanner. The PCs can also share application and data files easily and they can communicate using e-mail.

WAN

WAN = Wide Area Network

Computers connected over a long distance are part of a WAN. Large organisations may use a WAN to connect their offices in different parts of the country. For example, an organisation with branches in London, Cardiff, Leeds, Birmingham,

Glasgow and Edinburgh may have the offices connected using a WAN (the computers at each branch would be connected using a LAN). The WAN could use leased lines (perhaps from BT or Mercury) for the exclusive use of the organisation.

The advantages of linking PCs to a WAN is that data can be transferred a long distance very quickly (e.g. from your London office to your office in Edinburgh).

A computer linked to another via a modem over the telephone line would be part of a WAN. Computers linked via the Internet form a WAN. A PC attached to a WAN can have access to huge amounts of information (on the Internet) and communicate with others using e-mail (which is much quicker than sending information using the traditional mail service).

Modem

This device is used to link computers to the telephone line. It converts (modulates) the digital signal from the computer into an analogue wave that can be transmitted across the telephone network, then changes the signal back from analogue to digital at the other end (demodulates). It is usually fitted internally in the processor box. Modems work at speeds (known as the *baud rate*) from 14,400 bps (bits per second) up to 56,600 bps. Although faster modems cost more than slower ones there are potential savings to be made on your line costs through faster data transfer.

Modem = Modulator/ Demodulator

ISDN and PSDN

Instead of having a dedicated link between one LAN and another i.e. a WAN, it is possible to dial up digital connections as and when required. These connections are called *circuit-switched digital services.* The ISDN is an example of this type of system. This type of telephone link is much faster than the PSDN – the analogue network that you are probably connected to when you use your telephone or PC from home. A digital network transfers data much quicker than an analogue one, there is no need for a modem, and the data transferred is much less susceptible to corruption (data getting lost, etc.).

ISDN = Integrated Services Digital Network

PSDN = Public Switched Data Network

Internet

The Internet is a WAN of sorts. Computers from all over the world are linked together to form the Internet. To access the Internet you need:
- a computer linked to the telephone network via a modem;
- a browser, e.g. Internet Explorer or Netscape Navigator;
- an account with an Internet Service Provider (ISP).

World Wide Web (WWW)

The WWW is a vast collection of information stored on *Web pages* and on *Web sites*. Anyone connected to the Internet can view, read, print and/or download the information held on the WWW.

Search engine

The WWW contains a vast amount of information. To help users find the information they want on the WWW, a *search engine* can be used. There are several search engines to choose from, e.g. AskJeeves, AltaVista, Yahoo!, Excite. You can locate the search engines at their sites, e.g. www.askjeeves.co.uk.

When using a search engine you enter the word or phrase you are looking for into a text field – the search engine then produces a list of Web pages and sites that make reference to what you have searched for.

Depending on how specific you have been in entering your request, and depending on the search engine used, you may have a few sites suggested – or 100s or 1000s!

Electronic mail (e-mail)

If you have access to the Internet you can send e-mail messages to anyone else who is connected to it. You can send text, data, pictures, etc. Messages received can be read, replied to and forwarded to someone else, stored, printed or deleted as required. Everyone who uses e-mail has a unique address. E-mail is very quick and cheap and compares very favourably with the traditional mail service ('snail mail').

2
Using Windows

IN THIS CHAPTER:

- Start, shut down and restart your computer
- Desktop icons
- Working with windows
- Menus
- Control Panel
- Formatting diskettes
- Getting Help
- Accessories
- Shortcuts

You should work through this chapter at your computer. Manipulating Windows, customising your desktop, specifying your settings, creating shortcuts, etc. allow you to set up your computer the way that you want it to be. Try out the features discussed and experiment with the options. By the end of this chapter you'll be feeling more comfortable with the jargon and the Windows environment.

Start, shut down and restart your computer

Switching on the computer

Desktop – the work area displayed when you start Windows

The exact location of the on/off switch on a PC varies from model to model. Have a look at your PC and try to find the switch. The switch on the main unit (the box containing the hard drive, CPU, modem etc) is normally on the front of the unit. The switch for the VDU (if it has one) will most probably be on the front of the unit, but it may be up the side or even on the back.

① Ensure that your PC is plugged in and the power is switched on at the socket.

② Press the ON/OFF button on the main unit.

③ Switch on the screen (if necessary – with some PCs the screen goes on and off with the main unit).

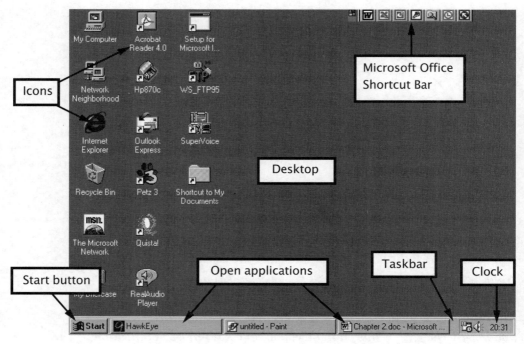

Some of the icons on your desktop may be different to the ones shown here.

④ Sit back and wait for a few seconds while your computer comes to life.

Your computer will display the *Desktop* ready for you to tell it what you want to do next.

Shut down the computer

When you have finished working on your computer it is important that you shut it down properly. If you don't shut the computer down properly you may get error messages the next time you boot up (switch on).

Try it: Shut down your computer

① Click the **Start** button on the Taskbar.

② Choose **Shut Down**.

③ Select *Shut down the computer?*

④ Click **Yes**.

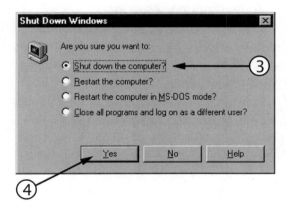

To restart the computer

When you are working in Windows, there may be occasions when your computer 'hangs' and refuses to do anything. When this happens it is impossible to shut the computer down in the normal way and start it again, so an alternative method must be used.

Don't use this method to shut down your computer when things are working fine – only use it when the computer refuses to respond to your instructions.

To restart the computer:

① Press the [Ctrl]-[Alt]-[Delete] keys (simultaneously).

② At the **Close Program** dialog box, press [Ctrl]-[Alt]-[Delete] again.

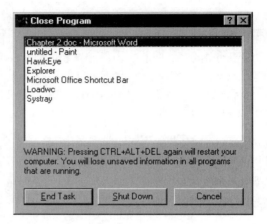

• Your computer will restart.

Very occasionally, your computer may not even respond to [Ctrl]-[Alt]-[Delete] – all you can do then is switch it off then switch it back on again! If this doesn't work you need technical assistance!

Desktop icons

Some of the icons on the desktop will have appeared automatically e.g. when Windows, Internet Explorer or an application was installed on your system. Other icons may have been put there manually by yourself (or some other user) to give a *shortcut* to an application, disk drive, folder or file on your system.

If the AutoArrange option is switched off, the icons on the Desktop can be moved around – simply drag and drop them with the mouse.

Try it: Arrange the Desktop icons

To switch the AutoArrange option on and off:

① Right-click anywhere on the Desktop (this displays a shortcut menu with options that you can choose from).

② Choose **Arrange Icons** (move the mouse pointer over the option).

③ Click **AutoArrange** to switch the option on or off.

When following instructions, **click** means use the left mouse button

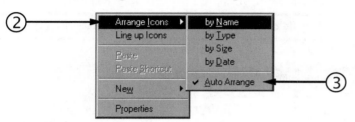

A tick beside the Auto Arrange options means that the option is switched on; no tick means it is off.

With the Auto Arrange option switched on, you can opt to sort the icons on your desktop by Name, Type, Size or Date.

① Right-click anywhere on the Desktop.

② Choose **Arrange Icons**.

③ Click the sort option – **By Name**, **Type**, **Size** or **Date**.

If AutoArrange is switched off, and you move some of the icons, you can line them up again by choosing **Line up Icons** in the shortcut menu. The icons line up with an invisible grid.

Working with windows

When you view the drives and folders on your PC using My Computer or Windows Explorer, the drives and folders (see Chapter 3) are displayed in a window.

When you open an application on your computer the application will be displayed in a window.

Let's have a look at a window using My Computer (don't worry if you don't understand everything that is displayed within the window, we're just looking at the basic structure of ALL windows).

① Double-click 🖳 on the Desktop.

• The *My Computer* window is opened.

My Computer and Windows Explorer will be discussed in the next chapter. In this chapter we are simply using them to help you identify the main areas found in any window.

It is important that you can recognise, name and know the purpose of the different parts of a window.

The main areas are labelled on the diagram:

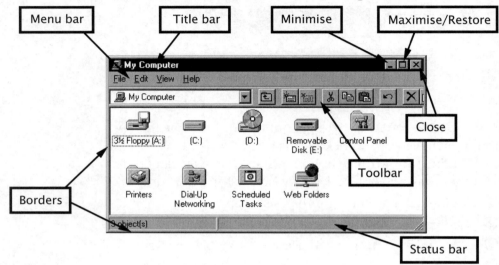

If a window is *maximised* it fills the whole screen – you cannot see any Desktop area behind it.

If a window is not maximised, you'll see some Desktop area behind it.

Try it: Resize a window

• You can toggle between a window being maximised or not by clicking the **Maximise/ Restore** button (or by double-clicking the window Title Bar).

• To minimise a window, click the **Minimise** button.

The titles of all open windows are displayed on the Taskbar. (To move from one window to another, simply click on its title on the Taskbar.)

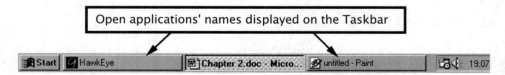

• To restore a minimised window click its Taskbar button.

Resize

If a window is not maximised you can see its border. You drag its border to make the window larger or smaller. The pointer becomes a double-headed arrow when over a border.

Move

Windows that are not maximised can be moved around the desktop. Click and drag the title bar of a window to move it.

Close

* To close a window, click the Close button ☒.

Have a look at some other windows and see if you can identify the different areas.

Close window –
click ☒ in top
right corner

Try it: Open Windows Explorer

① Right-click on the **My Computer** icon.

② Click on **Explore**.

Try to identify the areas described above.

Most windows have scroll bars on them. You use these to move up, down, right and left to display more information.

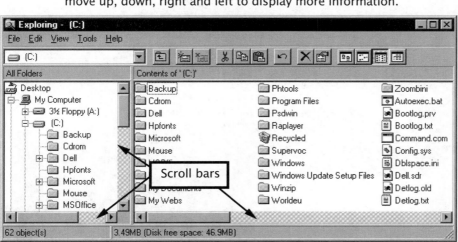

Have a look at WordPad (Start ▶ Programs ▶ Accessories ▶ WordPad), Paint (Start ▶ Programs ▶ Accessories ▶ Paint) or Solitaire (Start ▶ Programs ▶ Accessories ▶ Games ▶ Solitaire) and identify the different areas in the window.

▶ indicates the choice to make from a menu

If you have several windows open you can easily move from one window to another.

Try it: Move from one window to another

① Click on the title of the window you wish to move to on the Taskbar.

Or

② Hold down the [Alt] key and press [Tab].

◆ Keep the [Alt] key held down and press [Tab] repeatedly. You will cycle through the open windows. When the one you require is displayed on the screen, release the keys.

If you have several windows open, e.g My Computer, Paint, etc., you can tile or cascade them on your Desktop.

Try it: Tile and Cascade windows

① Right-click on an empty area of the Taskbar.

② Choose **Tile Horizontally**, **Tile Vertically** or **Cascade** from the shortcut menu.

Windows tiled vertically

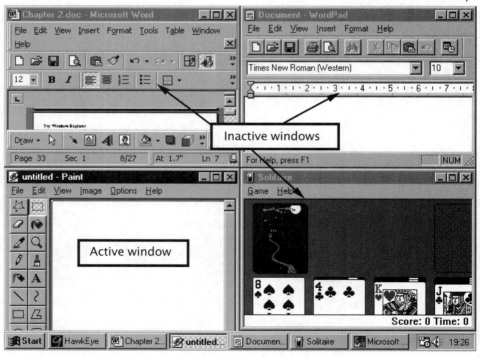

Windows may be active or inactive. The active window in this example has the dark title bar (blue on the screen), the inactive windows have grey title bars. To make a window active (so that you can work in it) click anywhere within it.

Active window – the window that you are working in

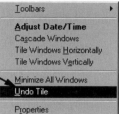

To undo the tile or cascade effect:

① Right-click on an empty area of the Taskbar.

② Click **Undo Tile** or **Undo Cascade**.

♦ Once you've finished experimenting with the layout, close all open windows and return to the Desktop.

Mouse techniques

Point	Move the mouse pointer until it is over the required area
Click	Press the left button once, and release immediately
Double-click	Press the left mouse button twice in close succession.
Drag	Click and hold down the left mouse button, move the mouse over the screen until the object is selected/moved etc.
Right-click	Press the right mouse button once, and release immediately

Menus

At the top of each window is a menu bar. You can use this to access every command in that window. You can display menus and select items using the mouse or the keyboard.

Using the mouse

① Click on the menu name to display the list of options available in that menu.

② Click on the menu item you wish to use.

• Menu items shown in black are 'active' (available for use).

• Inactive items are dimmed.

• Items with ellipses (...) at the end lead to a dialog box where you can specify options.

• An item with an arrow at the right side will display a submenu of related items.

Using the keyboard

- Hold down the [Alt] key and press the underlined letter in the menu name e.g. [Alt]–[F] for the File menu, [Alt]–[V] for the View menu.

Try it: Select an item from a menu:

- Keep the [Alt] key held down and press the underlined letter in the option required, e.g. **O** in the **File** menu to **Open**.

Or

- Use the up and down arrow keys until the item is selected, then press the [Enter] key.

Once a menu is displayed, you can press the right or left arrow keys to move from one menu to another.

Some commands have keyboard shortcuts that you can use instead of opening the menu and selecting the item. These are displayed on the right of the menu item.

Shortcut menus

Shortcut menu – displays the options most often used on the area clicked on

We've already discussed the desktop shortcut menu above, and the fact that there are options on it to help you position the icons on the desktop.

You can display and use shortcut menus in most windows. Simply *right*-click on an item or area, and the shortcut menu for that item or area will be displayed.

To close a menu without selecting an item from the list:

- Click the menu name again, click anywhere off the menu list or press the [Esc] key on your keyboard.

In addition to the menus, many of the commands can be initiated using the toolbars or keyboard shortcuts.

Control Panel

System Properties

You can see the components of your system, but there may be times when you need more specific information about your computer, e.g. when you need technical assistance, or are having problems with your hardware or wish to check whether a hardware or software upgrade/addition is appropriate.

If you need to check how much RAM your computer has, or what processor it has, you can easily find out. The information is listed in the System Properties dialog box.

Try it: Access information about your system

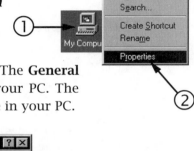

① Right-click on the **My Computer** icon.

② Choose **Properties**.

The **System Properties** dialog box will appear. The **General** tab contains basic system information about your PC. The **Device Manager** tab lists the items of hardware in your PC.

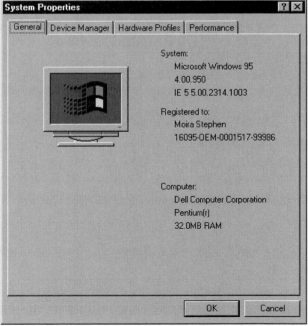

Click on the label at the top of a tab to bring it into view, e.g. click on **General** to see general information about your system.

A dialog box looks similar to a window, but if you should be able to spot a couple of basic differences.

- A dialog box has no Minimise, Maximise/Restore buttons – you can't change the size of a dialog box (but you can move it by dragging its title bar).

- A dialog box has an **OK** button and a **Cancel** button. If you make changes to the information that is in a dialog box, clicking **OK** will close the dialog box and make the changes take effect. If you click the **Cancel** button, the dialog box will close, but no changes will take effect.

In this example, the details regarding the computer's operating system, processor and RAM are:

- Windows 95
- Pentium Processor
- 32Mb RAM

Date and time

At the far right of the Taskbar you will notice the clock. If you move your mouse pointer over the clock, the current date will appear.

The date and time displayed on your clock should be accurate. If it isn't you can adjust the settings.

Try it: Set the date and/or time

① Open the **Start** menu.

② Choose **Settings**...

③ Click **Control Panel**.

④ Double-click .

Date/Time

At the Date/Time Properties dialog box, edit the settings as necessary.

On the Date & Time tab

To set the date:

① Select the month from the drop-down list (click the arrow on its right to open the list, then click on the month).

② Set the year (either use the split arrows to the right of the field to increase or decrease the values, or select the current entry and type in the year).

③ Click on the correct date.

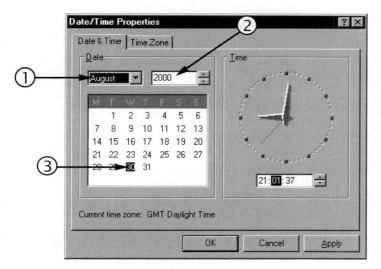

In a dialog box,
OK – apply the options selected and close the dialog box
Cancel – close the dialog box without applying any changes
Apply – apply the options selected but don't close the dialog box

To set the time:

④ Double-click on the part of the time field that you wish to change – the hours, minutes or seconds.

⑤ Use the split arrows to the right of the field to increase or decrease the value as necessary, or type in the value.

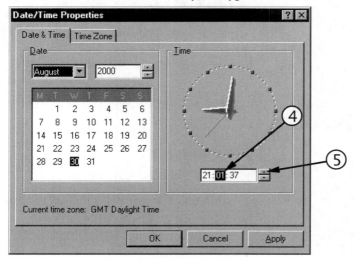

On the Time Zone tab

To change the time zone:

① Choose the time zone from the drop-down list.

• If you want to have your clock changed automatically each spring/autumn, select the checkbox.

② Click **OK**.

Display Properties

Background

The desktop on your computer can be customised in a variety of ways. For example, you can select a background design for your desktop from a list of *patterns* or *wallpapers*.

Try it: Choose a background

① Open the **Control Panel**.

② Double-click 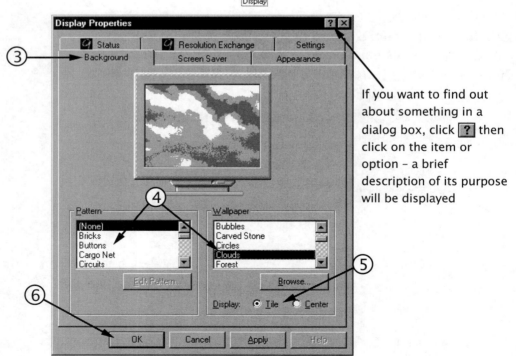.

If you want to find out about something in a dialog box, click ? then click on the item or option – a brief description of its purpose will be displayed

③ Select the **Background** tab.

④ Choose a pattern from the **Pattern** list or a wallpaper from the **Wallpaper** list

⑤ Select the display option required – **Tile** (to cover the whole Desktop with the pattern or wallpaper) or **Center** (to centre the selected image in the Desktop).

⑥ Click **OK**.

• You can also display this dialog box if you *right*-click on the Desktop, then left-click on Properties.

Screen Saver

Screen savers are designed to protect your screen from the damage that can occur if it has a static image on it for prolonged periods. A screen saver is either a moving image or a blank screen that limits the damage that can be done to your screen. If you have an energy-saving monitor that turns the display off when it is inactive, then a screen saver is not essential, but they can still be fun.

You'll find you've several screen savers to choose from, and they can be customised in a number of ways.

Try it: Change the screen saver

① Open the **Display Properties** dialog box.

② Select the **Screen Saver** tab.

③ Select the screen saver that you wish to use.

④ Click the **Settings**... button.

⑤ Customise the settings as required and click **OK**.

⑥ Click **Preview** to see how your screen saver looks.

• Repeat steps 3–6 as necessary until you are satisfied with your choice.

⑦ If you wish to password-protect your system, select the **Password protected** checkbox and click the **Change**... button.

⑧ Complete the **Change Password** dialog box as required and click **OK**.

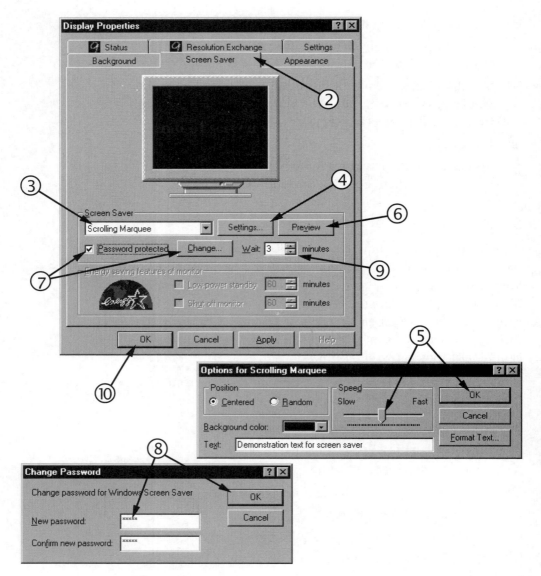

⑨ Set the **Wait** (the time that the screen is inactive before the screen saver cuts in) as required – something between 2 and 4 minutes is usually fine.

⑩ Click **OK**.

• Once the screen saver is set, it will appear on your screen any time that the PC is inactive for the time specified in the **Wait** field on the **Screen Saver** tab.

- When you move the mouse or press a key, the screen saver will close and your work will be displayed again.

- If you set a password, you have to enter it into a dialog box before you are allowed to access your work again.

- If you password-protect your screen saver DON'T FORGET THE PASSWORD!

If you have set a password then decide you wish to switch the facility off, return to the Screen Saver tab in the Display Properties and deselect the **Password protected** checkbox.

Appearance

If you don't like the standard colour scheme, or if someone has set a scheme that you don't like, you can easily change it.

Try it: Change the colour scheme

① Open the **Display Properties** dialog box and select the **Appearance** tab.

② Select the colour scheme required from the **Scheme:** list.

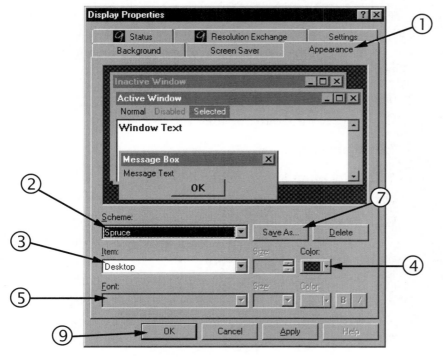

You can also create your own personal colour scheme.

③ Choose an item to customise from the **Item:** list.

④ Select a colour for the item from the **Color:** options.

⑤ If the selected item contains text, e.g. a Title Bar, select the font, size, colour, bold and italic options as required.

⑥ Repeat steps 3–5 for each item you wish to customise.

⑦ To save your colour scheme, click the **Save As...** button.

⑧ Give your scheme a name at the **Save Scheme** dialog box and click **OK**.

⑨ Click **OK** on the **Appearance** tab.

Your saved scheme will be included in the **Scheme:** list so you can easily apply the colours again (if someone changes the colour scheme of your display).

• If you decide that you prefer the default colour scheme, choose *Windows Standard* from the **Scheme** list.

Mouse

The mouse can be set up for right- or left-handed users. You can also specify the shape and size of the pointer, the speed at which it moves on the screen, whether or not it should have pointer trails, etc.

Try it: Specify the way your mouse works

① Display the **Control Panel**.

② Double-click .

To specify right- or left-hand operation:

③ Select the **Buttons** tab.

④ Click the **Button configuration** option required (prompts in the dialog box will tell you how the left and right mouse buttons work for each option).

⑤ Set the **Double-click speed** if required – use the test box to try out the different speeds.

To change the pointer options:

⑥ Select the **Pointers** tab.

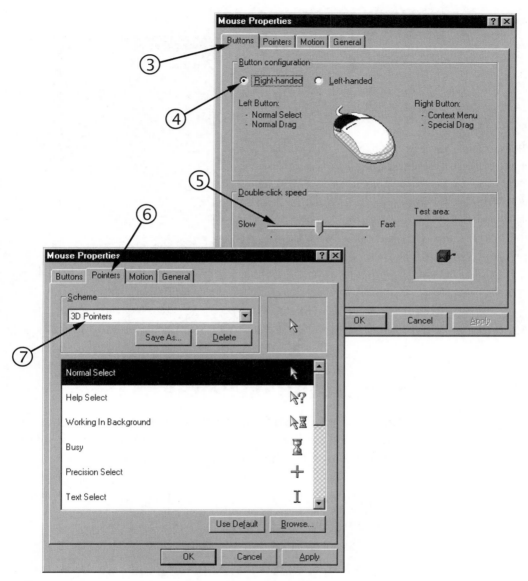

⑦ Choose a scheme from the **Scheme** list then click **OK**.

To adjust the pointer speed or switch pointer trails on and off.

⑧ Select the **Motion** tab.

⑨ Set the **Pointer speed** (drag the speed adjuster along the bar) and **Pointer trail** options as required.

⑩ Click **OK**.

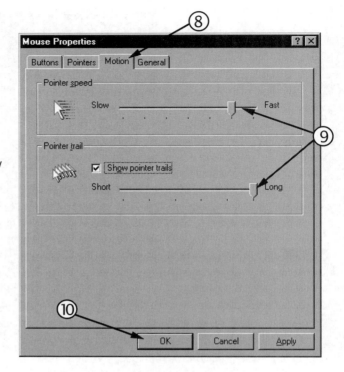

Pointer trails leave ghost images on screen for a few seconds – they make it easier to see where the pointer has gone

Formatting diskettes

Most of the time you will probably save your work to the hard drive (C:) or to a network drive (H, J, Y, etc.). There may be times however when you need to use a diskette, e.g.

*   in a school or college where you do not have storage space allocated to you on the hard drive or network drive.

*   to move information from one PC to another.

*   to take a copy of some data files for security purposes.

You can also format diskettes that have already been used. Those that have had a lot of use will benefit from a reformat. When you format diskettes that contain data, that data is lost (so be careful not to format one that contains something that you want to keep). It *may* be possible to recover data that has been lost through formatting, if you have the right software (which most users don't) – so my advice is *don't* format a disk that contains data unless you're quite sure.

To format a diskette:

① Insert the diskette into the diskette drive (A:) on your PC (metal part goes in first, label facing upwards if the drive is horizontal, label to the right if it is vertical).

② Double-click to start *My Computer*.

③ Right-click on then select **Format**...

Don't try to force a diskette into the drive – you may have it the wrong way round

④ Select the **Capacity** required. The default (1.44Mb) is for high-density (HD) diskettes (which most people use). For double-density (DD) diskettes set the capacity to 720Kb.

⑤ Specify the **Format type** – if the diskette hasn't been formatted before this must be set to Full. If the diskette is being reformatted you can choose Quick (erase).

⑥ Give your diskette a label (name) if you wish – a maximum of 11 characters is permitted.

⑦ Select the **Display summary when finished** checkbox.

⑧ Click **Start**.

• If your diskette has no errors on it the *total disk space* and *available disk space* figures should be the same. If there are faulty areas on it they will be indicated in the *bad sectors* figure. If the diskette is faulty – bin it!

Summary information is displayed once the formatting is complete

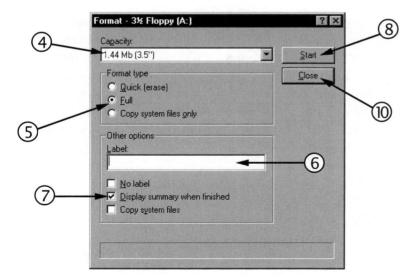

Diskettes must be formatted before you can store data on them.
You can buy disks pre-formatted.

⑨   Close the **Format Results (A:)** dialog box.

•   If you wish to format another diskette, remove the one you've just formatted, insert another diskette and repeat.

⑩   When you've finished, close the **Format (A:)** dialog box.

Startup disk

If you are responsible for the maintenance of your computer, you should have a *Startup disk.* I'd suggest you make two startup disks – just in case something happens to one of them!

Try it: Create a Startup disk as you format

①   Put a *high density* diskette in the A: drive.

②   Display the **Format – 3 ½ Floppy (A:)** dialog box.

③   Specify the format options as required – you could give your diskette a label, such as '*Windows Startup disk*'.

④   Select the **Copy system files** checkbox.

⑤   Click **Start**.

Put a label on the outside of your disk and write *Windows Startup disk* clearly on the label, then put the disk somewhere safe (preferably 'offsite') in case you ever need it.

Startup disk – a disk that can be used to start your system if you have problems starting Windows

You can also create a Startup disk from the **Add/Remove Programs** utility in the Control Panel

Windows Help

As you work with your PC there will be times (many times!) when you need help! You might find the answers in this book, or you could try the on-line Help system. It is very important that you learn to find your way around the Help system – in Windows and also in any applications that you use.

We will look at the Windows Help system here. Once you are familiar with one Help system you will very quickly find your way around any other.

Try it: Explore the on-line Help

①   Open the **Start** menu.

②   Choose **Help**.

•   The **Help Topics** dialog box opens. You can interrogate the system through the **Contents**, **Index** or **Find** tabs.

Contents tab

The easiest and the best way to have a browse through the Help system is from the Contents tab.

*   The Help topics are grouped into books or folders.
*   Sometimes a book will contain other books, sometimes it will contain the names of Help pages.

To open or close a book or folder, double-click on it

To display the contents of a page, double-click on it

To return to Help Topics, click **Help Topics** at the top of any Help page

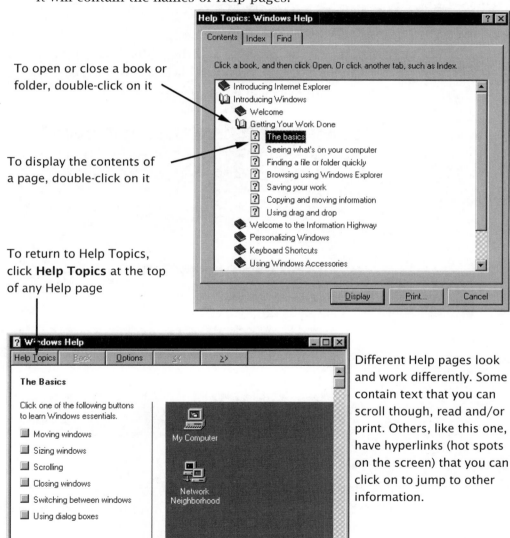

Different Help pages look and work differently. Some contain text that you can scroll though, read and/or print. Others, like this one, have hyperlinks (hot spots on the screen) that you can click on to jump to other information.

Index tab

If you know the word or topic that you want help on, you can use the **Index** tab.

① Type in the first few letters or words in the top part of the **Index** tab. The list of topics will scroll to bring into view topics starting with those letters.

② Double-click on the topic you want help on, or click on the topic and click **Display**.

④ You may be presented with another list of topics to choose from – just double-click on the one you want.

• The Help page will be displayed.

[F1] will call up the on-line Help in an application

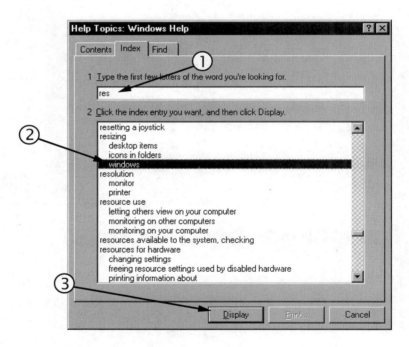

Find tab

The third option is to use the **Find** tab.

① Start typing the word(s) you want in the first slot in the **Find** tab.

② Select a matching word from the list to narrow your search.

③   Double-click on the topic in the lower list.

Or

④   Select a topic and click **Display**.

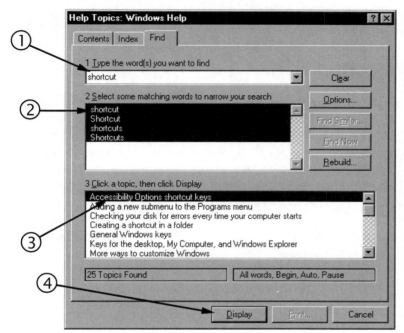

To display the on-line Help for any program, **open the Help menu** and **choose Help Topics**

Glossary items

Some Help pages contain glossary items – green text with a broken underline. These are jargon or technical terms. You can get a brief description of the term by clicking on the word or phrase in the Help window.

Retracing your steps

If you've moved through several Help pages, then decide that the information that you really needed was back a page or two, click Back until you get back to the page required.

Printing a Help topic

If you want to print a Help topic out:

①   Click Options at the top of the Help page.

②   Choose **Print Topic**... from the list.

③   Click **OK** at the Print dialog box.

Explore the Help system. You may not understand some of its topics, but get a feel for how it works and how to move around within it.

Accessories

There are several mini applications bundled with Windows. These can be accessed through the Accessories submenu (Start ▶ Programs ▶ Accessories). We won't discuss all of the Accessories – just some that may be useful initially, or that can provide a bit of fun!

Games

Several games are included in Windows. The standard ones are FreeCell, Hearts, Minesweeper and Solitaire.

Try it: Games

①   Start the game of your choice, e.g. *Solitaire* – Start ▶ Programs ▶ Accessories ▶ Games ▶ Solitaire.

•   Solitaire is just like the traditional card game Patience. If you have no-one to show you how the game works, try the on-line Help.

② Click ❌ to close the game when you've finished playing.

Calculator

If you need to do some quick calculations, there's a calculator ready to place on your desktop!

Try it: Calculator

① Start the Calculator – Start ▶ Programs ▶ Accessories ▶ Calculator.

② Click the buttons using the mouse – the figures and results will appear in the display area.

If you find the calulator useful, minimise it when not in use so that it is left open. Just click 〔📟 Calculator〕 on the Taskbar to display it again when required.

The Calculator can be used just like a normal pocket calculator – but it also has some extra functions. The **Back** button will erase the last digit or symbol entered. The **View** menu lets you switch between the full **Scientific** and the **Standard** mode.

Paint

If you are feeling a little artistic, try Paint. It's a bit basic, but your kids or grandkids will have a lot of fun with it!

Try it: Paint

① Start Paint – Start ▶ Programs ▶ Accessories ▶ Paint.

② Experiment with the drawing tools down the left of the screen or check out the on-line Help.

If you are proud of the masterpiece you create, you could use it as the Wallpaper on your desktop! You have to *save* the picture before you can do this.

Drawing toolbar

Try it: Save a picture

① Open the **File** menu.

② Choose **Save**.

③ Locate the folder you want to save the picture in.

④ Give the file a name.

⑤ Click **Save**.

To use a picture as Wallpaper:

① Open the **File** menu.

② Choose **Set As Wallpaper (Tiled)** – if you want to fill the screen with the picture, or **Set As Wallpaper (Centered)** – if you want the picture centred on the Desktop.

You can easily change the Wallpaper if you get tired of using your picture – see *Display Properties, Background* earlier in this chapter.

WordPad

WordPad is a basic word processing package. If you have Word or Works on your computer, you'll probably use them for your word processing requirements. If you haven't, WordPad is perfectly adequate if you need to produce some simple documents.

WordPad has its own Help files - check them out if necessary

Try it: WordPad

① Open WordPad (Start ▶ Programs ▶ Accessories ▶ WordPad)

• A new file is created automatically.

② Type in your document

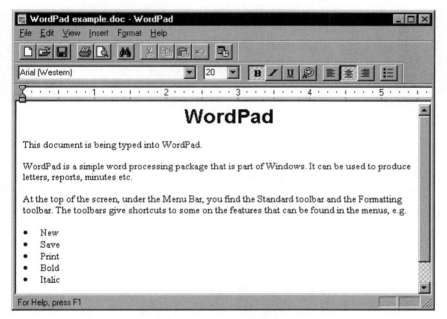

Key points

To correct mistakes:

• Use the [←] key (to delete a character to the left of the insertion point).

Or

• Use the **[Delete]** key (to delete a character to the right of the insertion point).

To save your file:

① Click 🖫 on the Standard toolbar.

Insertion point – flashing vertical bar in the document area. When you type, your text will appear at the insertion point

② In the **Save in:** slot, locate the folder to save it to.

③ Give your file a name.

④ Click **Save**.

See **Chapter 3** for information on locating folders and files on your system

To open an existing file:

① Click 📂 on the Standard toolbar.

② Locate the folder your file is in.

③ Select the file.

④ Click **Open**.

To create a new document:

① Click 📄 on the Standard toolbar.

② Select the New Document type, e.g. Word 6 Document.

③ Click **OK**.

To print one copy of the document:

• Click 🖨 on the Standard toolbar.

Selection techniques

If you want to format, copy or move existing text you must *select* the text first.

To select:

• *Any amount of text*, drag over the text with the mouse.

• *The whole document*, press [Ctrl]–[A].

To format selected text:

Toggle – click to switch on or off

Experiment with the tools on the formatting toolbar!

B toggles bold

I toggles italics

U toggles underline

10 ▾ changes the font size (click the down arrow and select the size from the drop-down list)

≣ centres ≣ right aligns ≣ left aligns a paragraph

To move or copy text:

① Select the text.

② Click ✂ to cut (to move), or 📋 to copy.

③ Place the insertion point where you want the text moved or copied to and click 📋.

Shortcuts

You can create shortcuts on the Desktop that take you to any drive, folder or file on your system.

If you use any of the Accessories regularly, e.g. Calculator, you might want to create a shortcut to it. You can then open the application by double-clicking on the shortcut, rather than having to go through all the menus each time. The calculator application can be found in the *Windows* folder – you're looking for the file called ***Calc.exe.***

Try it: Create a shortcut to a file

① Locate the file you wish to create a shortcut to (either in Windows Explorer or My Computer).

② Restore/resize the window if necessary – so that you can see your Desktop as well as the window.

③ Right-click on the file, drag it onto the Desktop and release the mouse button.

④ At the shortcut menu click **Create Shortcut(s) Here.**

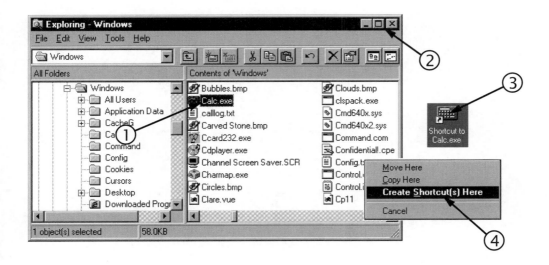

3
File management

IN THIS CHAPTER:

- Disks and drives
- Folders
- File types
- Searching for files
- Backups
- Viruses

This chapters discusses file management. You will learn about folders and files and how you can organise them on your disks. We will discuss some of the different types of file, and suggest methods that can help you locate files if you think you've lost them! You will also learn how to copy and backup files – procedures which offer you some protection against the inconvenience that can result from lost data. Viruses, and how to protect your system from them, are also discussed.

Disks and drives

Disks may be fixed e.g. the disk in the C: drive, or removable e.g. diskettes, CDs and zip disks

The programs and data that are stored on your PC are held on disks which are housed in drives. The drives are named using letters of the alphabet. Your diskettes use the A: drive (and the B: drive if you have two). Your local hard drive is the C: drive. Your CD-ROM drive is probably your D: drive. You may have other drives, e.g. Zip drives for backups or network drives, available to you. They will be named E:, F:, G:, H:, etc.

Key points: disks and drives

Disk   the main storage device on a PC;

Drive   a device that houses a disk – there are hard drives, diskette drives, Zip drives, CD drives, etc.;

Fixed disk   not removable – if you have one fixed disk it is probably in your C: drive;

Removable disk one that you can remove from your PC, e.g. a diskette, CD, DVD, Zip disk;

Floppy disk   another name for a diskette.

We have already seen that you can display the contents of your computer system and disks either through My Computer or by opening Windows Explorer (pages 27 – 30).

The structure of drives and folders is very hierarchical. At the first level in My Computer, the drives are displayed. Each drive is identified by a letter (A:, C:, D:, E: etc.).

My Computer seen in the large icons view

Double click on a drive to display its contents – you will find folders and/or files

Some of the folders have sub-folders, and some of these have sub-folders (folders are sometimes called directories).

When you are looking at your drives and folders through My Computer, you can see the contents of *one* drive, or *one* folder, at a time.

If you look at your drives and folders in Windows Explorer, you can see the folder structure and sub-structures of several drives and folders at the same time, in the left pane of the Exploring window.

When you select a drive or folder, its contents are displayed in the right pane

Windows Explorer displaying files and folders using the List view

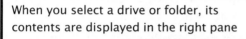

Click the + beside a drive or folder to expand its structure

Click the – beside a drive or folder to collapse its structure

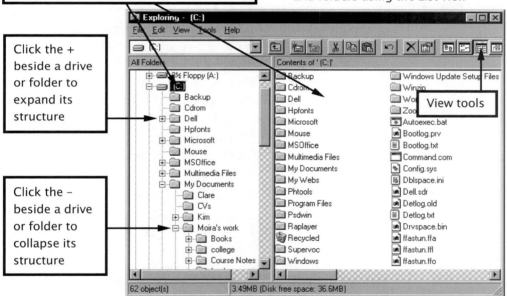

View tools

View options

In both My Computer and Windows Explorer there is the same *Standard* toolbar.

In Windows 95, the last four tools on the Standard toolbar change the way in which the folders and files are displayed – try them out and see which view you prefer.

In Windows 98/Me, you have the same View options, but here they are on a list that drops down from the View button.

Folders

Creating folders

Do not modify
the organisation
of folders that
contain
applications and
system software.
Restrict your
activities to within
My Documents, or
within a folder
you set up
yourself.

You can organise the folders that you use for your *data* files as you wish. You should give careful consideration to the folder structure that you use for storing your data files – the files that contain your letters, reports, budgets, etc.

If you are using Microsoft Office, the default location for your data files is the folder called *My Documents*.

You may use a different folder for your data – you could create one called *My Work* for example. You can easily create folders to help you organise the data files that you will create.

You can create a folder at drive level – immediately under the drive icon C: or A:, etc., or you can create a folder within an existing folder.

Let's say you decided to create a folder on the C: drive for your work. You could create a folder, giving it a name that reflects its contents, e.g. *My Work*. You could then set up other folders within your main folder for the different areas of your work. The structure could be something like this:

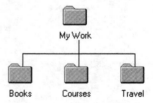

This structure could be created and modified in either My Computer or Windows Explorer.

Try it : Work with folders in My Computer

To display your drives and folders in My Computer

- Double-click on the My Computer icon on the desktop to see what drives you have access to.

To check the contents of any folder in My Computer:

- Double-click on the folder.

To display your drives and folders in Windows Explorer

① Right-click on **My Computer** on the Desktop.

② Click **Explore**.

Working in Windows Explorer

You can collapse or expand the view you have of your computer system in the left pane of the Explorer window.

- Click the + icon beside a drive, folder or My Computer to expand it to the next level.

- Click the – icon (displayed when a drive or folder is expanded) to collapse the display.

- If you click on a drive or folder in the left pane, its contents will be displayed in the right pane. Folders are listed first, then the files.

- You can change the way the contents of a drive or folder are displayed by using the View tools on the toolbar.

To create a folder directly under the C: drive:

① Double-click on the **C:** drive icon to display its contents.

Or

- Select the C: drive in the left pane (it doesn't matter if the folder structure has been expanded or not).

② Open the **File** menu.

③ Choose **New**, then **Folder**.

④ A new folder will appear in the window.

⑤ Type in the name that you want the folder to have, e.g. *My Work*, (to replace the *New Folder* name).

⑥ Press **[Enter]**.

To create a folder within this new folder:

① Double-click the *My Work* folder to open it.

Or

- In the left pane, select the folder (expand the C: drive if necessary) that will be the parent of the new folder

② Repeat steps 2 to 6 above.

You can set up folders on your computer to help you organise your work

To display different folder or file attributes:

• Click the **Details** tool at the right of the Explorer or My Computer toolbar.

To rename a folder or file:

① Select the folder or file.

② Open the **File** menu.

③ Choose **Rename**.

④ Type in the new name for the folder.

⑤ Press **[Enter]**.

File types

While exploring your folders, you may have noticed that not all files have the same extension (the three characters after the filename).

Different file types are created by different applications. Your extension at the end of a filename will indicate (or at least suggest) the application that the file was created in. Some of the common file types are listed here:

Extension	Application	File type
mdb	Access	Database
doc	Word	Word processing
xls	Excel	Spreadsheet
bmp	Paint	Image file
pub	Publisher	Desktop publishing
ppt	PowerPoint	Presentation graphics
htm	Various	Web page
rtf	Various	Word processing

FIle extensions are not always displayed. To show or hide them, open the **View** menu and choose **Options**. (In Windows Me, use **Folder Options** on the **Tools** menu.) Select or deselect the **Hide file extension** option as required and click **OK**.

You can check the type of any file if you display the file properties.

Try it: Display a file's properties

① Right-click on the file.

② Choose **Properties** from the shortcut menu.

③ The file type is displayed on the **General** tab.

④ Click **OK** to close the dialog box.

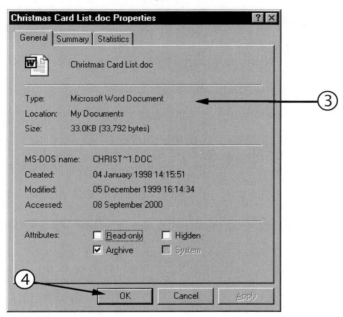

The Properties dialog box also displays other information about the file, e.g. date created, when it was last modified, its size, etc.

Copy, move and delete folders and files

As time goes by the number of data folders and files on your system will increase. At some stage you might decide that you want to modify the folder structure that you initially set up, or get rid of some files that you no longer require.

If you wish to copy, move or delete a folder or file the first thing that you must do is select it. It doesn't matter if you use My Computer or Windows Explorer for this, the technique is the same.

To select an individual folder or file:

- Click on it.

To select a group of adjacent folders or files:

① Click on the first folder or file.

② Hold the **[Shift]** key down.

③ Click on the last folder or file that you want to select.

To select several non-adjacent files or folders:

① Click on the first folder or file.

② Hold the **[Ctrl]** key down.

③ Click on each of the other files or folders as required.

Once you've selected your folder(s) or file(s) you can copy, move or delete them.

In Windows Me, Explorer has **Move To** and **Copy To** tools, offering simpler ways to move and copy files and folders

To copy a folder(s) or file(s):

① Select the folder(s) or file(s).

② Open the **Edit** menu and choose **Copy**, or click on the toolbar.

③ Select the folder or drive you wish to copy the folder or file(s) into.

④ Open the **Edit** menu and choose **Paste**, or click .

To move a folder(s) or file(s):

① Select the folder(s) or file(s).

② Open the **Edit** menu and choose **Cut**, or click 🖾.

③ Select the folder or drive you wish to copy the folder or file(s) into.

④ Open the **Edit** menu and choose **Paste**, or click 🖾.

To copy or move a folder or file(s) onto a diskette:

① Select the folder(s) or file(s).

② Open the **Edit menu** and **choose Copy or Cut** (depending on whether you wish to copy or move the folder or file(s)), or click 🖾 or 🖾.

③ Select the diskette drive.

④ Open the **Edit menu** and **choose Paste**, or click ▣.

To delete a folder(s) or file(s):

① Select the folder(s) or file(s).

② Press **[Delete]** on your keyboard.

③ At the **Confirm Folder Delete** or **Confirm File Delete** prompt click **Yes**.

Deleted files and folders are placed in a special folder called the Recycle Bin. You will find it listed amongst the folders on your C: drive.

Key points: Copy, move and delete

Copy	The file or folder (with all its contents) remains at its original location and a *copy* is duplicated at the destination.
Move	The file or folder (with all its contents) is moved to a new location.
Delete from HDD	Files and folders are placed in the Recycle Bin.
Delete from diskette	Files and folders are deleted immediately – *not* placed in the Recycle Bin.
Restore	Files and folders can be recovered (restored) from the Recycle Bin.

Deleting is a two step process. When you delete a folder or file from a hard drive it is placed in the Recycle Bin. Files and folders can be recovered from the Bin until it is emptied.

Recycle Bin

If you accidentally delete a file you can easily restore it (provided it's still in the Recycle Bin). The Recycle Bin is displayed on your Desktop and within the Desktop in Windows Explorer.

Try it: Use the Recycle Bin

To open the Recycle Bin:

• Double-click on it on the Desktop, or select it in the left pane of the Exploring window.

To recover file(s) from the Recycle Bin:

① Select the file(s) in the Recycle Bin.

② Open the **File menu** and choose **Restore**.

To empty the Bin without opening it, right-click on it on the Desktop then choose **Empty Recycle Bin** from the shortcut menu

Or

*   Right-click on the selected file(s) and choose **Restore** from the **Shortcut** menu.
③   The file(s) will be returned to their original folders.

To empty the Recycle Bin:

①   Open the **File** menu.
②   Choose **Empty Recycle Bin**.
③   Click **Yes** at the prompt.

*   Close the Recycle Bin when you've finished with it, or select a different drive or folder.

Searching for folders or files

If you have forgotten which folder you put your file into, you should be able to find it using the **Find** command in Windows Explorer.

In Windows Me, the **Find** routine has been replaced by **Search**, which is run in the Explorer Bar

①   Open the **Tools** menu.
②   Choose **Find**, then **Files or Folders**.

To search for a file or folder using its name:

①   Select the **Name & Location** tab.
②   Type in the name or the file or folder (or part of it if you don't know it all). The names are not case-sensitive.

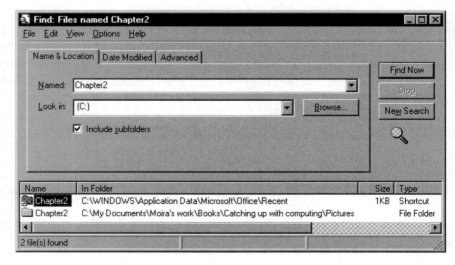

③ Select the drive that you want searched (or click **Browse** and locate the drive and/or folder you want to search).

④ Select or deselect the **Include subfolders** checkbox as required.

⑤ Click [Find Now].

To clear one set of search criteria before specifying the next set, click on [Ne_w Search]

A list of files or folders that match your search criteria will be displayed.

Key points: wildcard characters

If you don't know the exact spelling or name of the file/folder you are searching for you can use *wildcard characters* to replace some of the detail.

*	represents a string of characters
?	represents a single character
the might find	o*the*r, *the*re, *the*refore, bro*the*r
b?t might find	bit, but, bat, bet

To search for a file using date criteria:

① Select the **Date Modified** tab.

② Specify the date option required.

③ Click [Find Now].

You can give details on any combination of the three tabs when searching. Once you've found the file that you're looking for, you can open it by double-clicking on it in the **Name** list in the **Find** dialog box

To search by file type:

① Select the **Advanced** tab.

② Choose the **File Type** required in the **Of type** list.

③ Complete the **Containing text:** field as required.

④ Specify the size (if known).

⑤ Click [Find Now].

Backups

It is very important that you keep copies (or backups) of any important data that you have on your computer.

If you have all of your data stored on your C: drive, and then the drive becomes damaged or your PC gets stolen, you will have lost your data. At the very least this situation may be inconvenient; however, if it's business or work data, then it could be very serious indeed.

Always take a backup copy of important data

If you don't have many important data files (by important data files I mean any that you would be upset to lose!), you could just copy them onto a diskette (see copying files earlier in this chapter).

If you have a lot of files, you could use a Zip drive, or CD-RW for your copies.

Computer viruses

A virus is a piece of software that has been written with the specific purpose of causing havoc on computer systems. The software is called a virus because it has been programmed to spread through a system and then on to others, just like an infectious virus spreads through the general population.

Some viruses are harmless – they do no serious damage to your system, but serve to remind you just how vulnerable it may be.

Other viruses can have disastrous effects – deleting files, corrupting disks, etc.

No computer is immune to virus attack (although there aren't too many mainframe viruses), but some basic safety precautions can help limit the chances of infection.

Key points: anti-virus precautions

- Install reliable anti-virus software on your computer, and update it regularly
- Use the anti-virus software regularly to scan the system for viruses
- Use the anti-virus software to scan any removable disks before you open files on them
- Scan any files downloaded from the Internet before you open them – viruses are often transmitted in attachments to e-mails
- Install only genuine software from reputable sources

4
Standard features

IN THIS CHAPTER:

- Opening and closing applications
- File handling
- Help with applications
- Selection techniques
- Delete, Cut, Copy and Paste
- Spelling and grammar
- Formatting
- Preview and printing
- Drawing, pictures and WordArt
- Toolbars

Many of the skills that you use within an application, such as Word, work in the same or very similar ways in other applications. This chapter discusses these common skills. You should read through this chapter before going to the chapters which discuss the individual tasks, and refer back to here as necessary.

Opening and closing applications

Many of the tools on the Standard and Formatting toolbars are the same in each application

In Chapter 2 we looked at opening some of the mini-applications that are part of Windows, e.g. Paint, Solitaire and WordPad. You can open other applications in the same way.

Try it: Start from the Start Menu

① Click the **Start** button on the **Taskbar**.

② Choose **Programs**.

③ Click the application, opening its menu first if necessary, e.g. Microsoft Excel; Accessories ▶ WordPad; Accessories ▶ Games ▶ Solitaire.

If you have Microsoft Office, you can use the Shortcut bar as an alternative to the Start menu to open an application.

Try it: Start from the Shortcut bar

• Click the tool for the application on the Shortcut bar.

Try it: Close an application

• Click the **Close** button ☒ at the right of the application's Title bar.

Key points in the application window

You should be able to recognise the following items:

• Title Bar   • Menu Bar   • Border
• Minimise   • Maximise/Restore   • Close button
• Toolbars, e.g. Standard, Formatting   • Status Bar

File handling

No matter what application you are in, the methods used to create, save, open and close files are very similar.

Try it: Create a new file

To create a new file using the default template:

• Click the **New file** tool ☐ on the **Standard** toolbar.

A new file will appear, e.g. *Document2*, *Book2*, (the number in the file name depends on the number of files you have created in this working session), or in some applications, e.g. Access, you will see a dialog box where you can provide additional information about the file you wish to create.

Save

If you want to keep your file, you must save it. If you don't, it will be lost when you exit your application. You can save your file at any time – you don't have to wait until you've finished.

*You can use long filenames. The path, e.g. C:\My Documents, filename and extension can add up to a maximum of 255 characters. Names can contain letters, numbers spaces and any other characters except these: / | \ > < * ? " : ;*

Try it: Save your file (see page

① Click the **Save** tool 🖫 on the **Standard** toolbar.

② At the **Save As** dialog box select the folder you want to save your file into (the default is the Desktop in WordPad, My Documents in Office applications).

③ Give your file a name.

④ Leave the **Save as type:** at the default, e.g. *Word Document* in Word, *Microsoft Excel Workbook* in Excel, *Word for Windows 6.0* in WordPad.

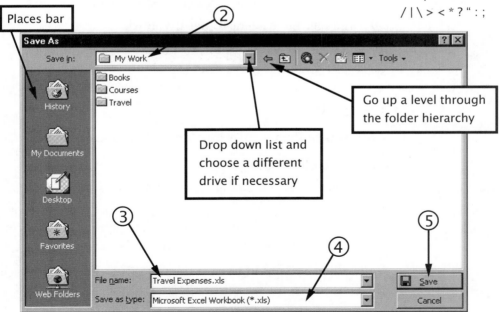

Places bar

Go up a level through the folder hierarchy

Drop down list and choose a different drive if necessary

⑤   Click **Save**.

•   The name of your file will appear on the Title bar in place of the temporary filename.

•   As your file develops, you can resave it any time – just click the **Save** tool 🖫 again. The **Save As** dialog box will not reappear, but the old version of the file on your disk will be replaced by the new, up-to-date version.

Save As

There may be times that you save a file, edit it, then decide that you want to save the edited file but also keep the original version of the file on disk.

If you don't want to overwrite the old file with the new version, you should save it using a different filename or to a different drive and/or folder. You can do this by opening the **Save As** dialog box from the **File** menu.

Try it: Save your file using a different filename or to a different location

①   Open the **File** menu and choose **Save As**.

②   The **Save As** dialog box will appear again.

③   Change the drive or folder if you wish.

④   Enter a new name in the **File name** field.

⑤   Click **Save**.

Close file

Once you've finished working on a file you should close it.

Try it: To close your file

•   Open the **File** menu and choose Close.
Or

•   **Click** the **Close** button ☒ at the top right of the file window (document, workbook, etc.) Title bar.

You will be prompted to save the file if it has changed since the last time you saved it.

Open a file

If you want to view, update or print a file that you have already created, saved and closed you must open it first.

Try it: Open an existing file

① Click the **Open** tool 🖱 on the **Standard** toolbar.

- The **Open** dialog box will appear on your screen.

② Locate the drive and/or folder in which your file is stored (see Key points below).

③ Select the file you wish to open – click on its name.

④ Click **Open**.

- You can also open a file by double-clicking on its name in the **Open** dialog box.

If the file is a recently used one, you will find its name displayed at the bottom of the File menu. You can open your file from here – just click on the name.

Key points to note in Save As and Open dialog boxes

To move to a folder at a lower level than the current one:

- Double-click on the folder in the file list.

To move to a folder at a higher level:

- Click 🗁 or press **[Alt]–[2]**.

To return to the My Documents folder from any other folder:

- Click 📁 My Documents on the **Places** bar.

If you have more than one file open, you will see the filenames displayed on the Taskbar at the bottom of your screen. If you point to the filename on the Taskbar, the full file name and the name of the application will be displayed.

- To move from one file to another, click on the file name that you want to display.

- Within an application, you can use the **Window** menu to go from one open document to another – you will find a list of your open documents at the end of it. Just click on the document you want to display.

If you wish to open more than one file simultaneously, select the files in the **Open** dialog box, then click **Open**.

Key points: Selecting files

To select a group of adjacent files:

① Click on the first file or folder.

② Hold the [Shift] key down.

③ Click on the last file or folder.

To select several non-adjacent files:

① Click on the first file or folder.

② Hold the [Ctrl] key down.

③ Click on each of the other files or folders as required.

MS Office Help

The Help system in many Windows applications works in a similar way to Windows Help – see Chapter 2.

Many of you are probably using Microsoft Office, so this section discusses that Help system. There are several ways of getting help – most of them very intuitive and user-friendly. The system works in the same way in all Office applications.

Try it: Use the Office Assistant

① Press **[F1]** or click the application Help tool 🔲 on the toolbar.

• The Assistant will display a list of topics that you might be interested in.

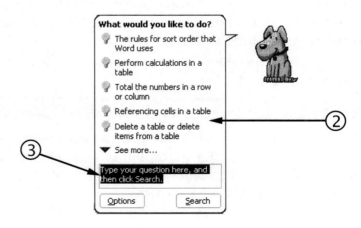

② To choose from the '*What would you like to do?*' list, simply click on the topic.

③ If you have a specific question you want to ask, type it in at the prompt and click the **Search** button.

• The Assistant will display the Help page.

Key points: Working in Help

Some pages contain text in a different colour – usually blue.

• Coloured text listed at the top of a Help page indicates a link to a different area in the current page.

• Coloured text embedded within the main text on a page is probably a phrase or some jargon that has an explanation or definition attached to it. Simply click the coloured text to display the definition.

• Any related Help pages are cross-referenced at the end of the page – to display a related page click on its link.

• Links that have been used change colour, usually to violet.

• Click the Close button ☒ to exit the Help system when you've finished with it.

The Office Assistant can remain visible as you work on your document, or you can hide it and call on it as required. If you opt to leave it displayed, drag it to an area of your screen where it doesn't obscure your work.

• If you leave the Office Assistant displayed, left-click on it any time you want to ask a question.

• To hide the Office Assistant, right-click on it and choose **Hide** from the pop up menu.

• To change the way the Office Assistant works, right-click on it and choose **Options** from the pop-up menu. Set the options required in the Office Assistant dialog box.

Tips

The Office Assistant is constantly monitoring your actions. If it thinks that it has a tip that may be useful to you, a light bulb will light up beside it. To read its tip, click the bulb.

Explore the on-line Help system. It's full of useful stuff, and you'll find the answers to most of your questions there

You can switch the Office Assistant off in the Office Assistant dialog box

Accessing Help

Whether or not you opt to use the Office Assistant, the application Help tool will open the on-line Help system. You can also access the Help system from the Help menu.

You can interrogate the Help system using the **Contents**, **Answer Wizard** or **Index** tabs.

- Click the 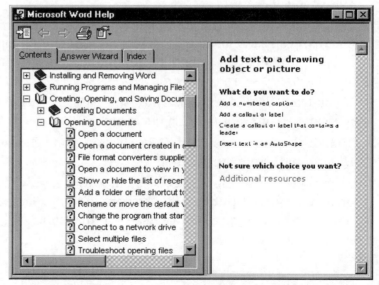 tool (on the toolbar in the Help window) to toggle the display of the tabs.

Contents tab

You can browse through the system from the Contents tab.

- Click the + to the left of a book to display or the – to hide its list of contents. When a book is open, you will be presented with another list of books, or a list of topics.

To display a topic:

① Click on it.

② Work through the Help system until you find the help you need.

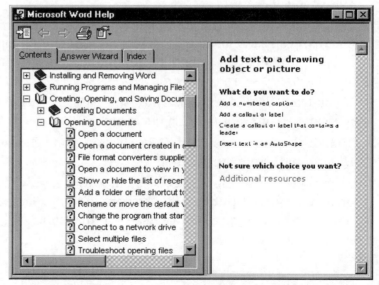

To print a topic:

- **Click** the **Print** tool ![printer icon] when the topic is displayed.

To revisit pages you've already been to:

- Click the **Back** tool ⇦ or **Forward** tool ⇨ to go back and forward through the pages.

Answer Wizard

You can ask questions on the Answer Wizard tab.

① Enter your question, e.g. '*How do I create a table*', and click **Search**.

② Select a topic from the **Select topic to display** list.

- The Help page will be displayed.

Index tab

If you know what you are looking for, the Index tab gives you quick access to any topic and is particularly useful once you are familiar with the terminology used in your application.

① At the **Help** dialog box, select the **Index** tab.

② Type the word you're looking for in the **Type keywords** field and click **Search**.

Or

③ Double-click on a word in the **Or choose keywords** list.

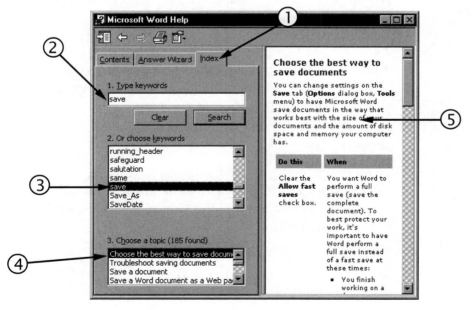

④   Choose a topic from the **Choose a topic** list.

⑤   Work through the system until you find what you need.

What's This?

If you haven't used Microsoft Office products before, or if you're new to the Windows environment, there will be many tools, menus, buttons and areas on your screen that puzzle you. The *What's This?* feature can help you here – it works best when a file is open, as most of the tools, menus and screen areas are then active.

Try it: Use What's This?

To find out what a tool does:

①   Hold down the **[Shift]** key and press **[F1]**.

②   Click the tool that you want information about.

To find out about an item in a menu list:

①   Hold down the **[Shift]** key and press **[F1]**.

②   Open the menu list and select the option required from the list.

To find out about anything else within an application window:

①   Hold down the **[Shift]** key and press **[F1]**.

②   Click on the item.

If you accidentally invoke the *What's This* help option or if you have read the information and wish to cancel it, press **[Shift]-[F1]** (or the **[Esc]** key) to continue.

ScreenTips

If you point to any tool on a displayed toolbar, a ScreenTip will probably appear to describe the purpose of the tool.

If no ScreenTips appear, the Show ScreenTips option has been switched off.

To switch ScreenTips on or off:

①   Point to any toolbar that is displayed and click the right mouse button.

②   Choose **Customize**... from the shortcut menu.

③   In the **Customize** dialog box select the **Options** tab.

④   To switch ScreenTips on, select the **Show ScreenTips on toolbars** option (if you don't like ScreenTips, deselect this option to switch them off).

⑤   Click **Close**.

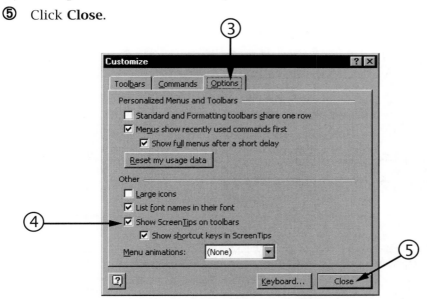

Dialog box Help

When you access a dialog box in an application, e.g. the Customize one above, you can get help on any item within it that you don't understand.

To get help on an item in a dialog box:

①   Click the **Help** button 🔲 on the dialog box title bar.

②   Click on an option, button or item in the dialog box that you want explained.

•   A brief explanation of the option, button or item you click on will be displayed.

③   Click anywhere within the dialog box to cancel the explanation.

Selection techniques

You must select your text or data before you can:

- Delete it (if you want to delete more than one character at a time)
- Format it
- Copy or move it

There are a several different methods that can be used to select, many of which are similar across the applications.

To select:

Any amount of text or data	Click and drag over it
Any amount of text, or adjacent cells	Click at beginning of text, hold [Shift] down, click at end of text or data
A line or row	Single-click to the left of the line or row
A character, cell or line a time	Hold the [Shift] key down and press the right, left, at up or down arrow keys
Paragraph	Double-click in the selection bar (down the left of the document area)
The whole document or worksheet	[Ctrl]-[A]
To the beginning of the document or worksheet	[Shift]-[Ctrl]-[Home]
To the end of the document or worksheet	[Shift]-[Ctrl]-End]
A picture or chart	Click on it

Key points: Selecting text

Selection techniques that are application-specific will be discussed in the relevant chapter

- Not all selection techniques work exactly the same in each application – experiment with them.

- Look for topics like "Selection techniques" or "Select text with the mouse" or "Select text with the keyboard" or "Select objects", etc. in the on-line Help to get specific details for individual applications.

To deselect any unit of text:

- Click anywhere within your text, or press one of the arrow keys on your keyboard.

Delete, Cut, Copy and Paste

Delete

If you have a large piece of text or data to delete, it will usually be quicker to select it and then press [Delete], rather than press [←] or [Delete] repeatedly.

Try it: Delete a chunk of text or data

① Select the text or data.

② Press **[Delete]**.

Cut, Copy and Paste

There will be times when you have entered the correct information into a file but it is in the wrong place. When this happens you should move or copy the object, e.g. text in Word, data in cells in Excel, a picture or graph in any application, to the correct location.

• If you want to remove an object from its current position, and place it somewhere else within your file you can *move* it from one place to another.

• If you want to keep the object, but repeat it in another place in your file (or in another file), you can *copy* it.

You can move or copy an object within or between files. Before you can move or copy something you must select it.

Try it: Cut (move) and copy text

① Select the text, data or object that you want to move.

② Click the **Cut** tool ✂ to move *or* the **Copy** tool 📋 to copy (they're on the Standard toolbar).

③ Position the insertion point where you want the object to reappear.

④ Click the **Paste** tool 📋 on the **Standard** toolbar.

• The object will appear at the insertion point.

Useful keyboard shortcuts
[Ctrl]-[X] to cut,
[Ctrl]-[C] to copy,
[Ctrl]-[V] to paste

In Office 2000 the Clipboard can hold up to 12 entries. You can show the Clipboard toolbar (see page 93) and paste whichever entry is required.

Key points when moving and copying

- Anything you cut or copy is placed in an area of memory called the *Clipboard.*

- The contents of the Clipboard are overwritten each time something is cut or copied to it.

- You can paste the contents of the Clipboard as often as you wish.

- The Clipboard is cleared when you exit Windows.

Try it: Cut or copy to a different file

① Open the file you want to move or copy the object from (the source file).

② Open the file you want to move or copy the object to (the destination file).

③ Display the file you want to move or copy from.

④ Select the object you want to move or copy.

⑤ Click the **Cut** [✂] or **Copy** [📄] tool on the **Standard** toolbar.

⑥ Display the file you want to move or copy the object to.

⑦ Position the insertion point where you want the object to go.

⑧ Click the **Paste** tool [📋] on the **Standard** toolbar.

Drag and drop

The contents of the Clipboard are not affected when you use this technique.

As an alternative to using Cut or Copy and Paste techniques to move and copy objects, you may find *drag and drop* useful.

Drag and drop is especially useful when moving or copying an object a short distance – i.e. to somewhere else on the screen. If you try to drag and drop over a longer distance, you will probably find that your file scrolls very quickly on the screen and that it is difficult to control.

Try it: Move or copy using drag and drop techniques

① Select the object that you want to move or copy.

② Position the mouse pointer anywhere over the selected object.

To move the object:

③ Click and hold down the left mouse button (notice the 'ghost' insertion point that appears within the selected area).

④ Drag the object and 'drop' it into its new position.

To copy the object:

① Select the object and point to it.

② Hold down your **[Ctrl]** key.

③ Click the object and hold down the left mouse button.

④ Drag the object and 'drop' it into its new position.

⑤ Release the **[Ctrl]** key.

Spelling and grammar

To help you produce accurate work, you can check the spelling and grammar in your document.

You can either:

• Let the application check your spelling and grammar as you work (in Word and PowerPoint). These options can be switched on and off in the **Options** dialog box (accessed through the Tools menu). In Word, the option is on the Spelling and Grammar tab, in PowerPoint it is on the Spelling and Style tab.

Or

• You can run a spell check at any time that suits you (in all applications)

Checking spelling and grammar as you type

This option is operational by default in Word and PowerPoint – if it doesn't work on your PC, someone has switched it off.

Words that aren't recognised will be underlined with a red, wavy line.

Any words, phrases or sentences that have unusual capitalisation or aren't grammatically correct will have a grey or green wavy line.

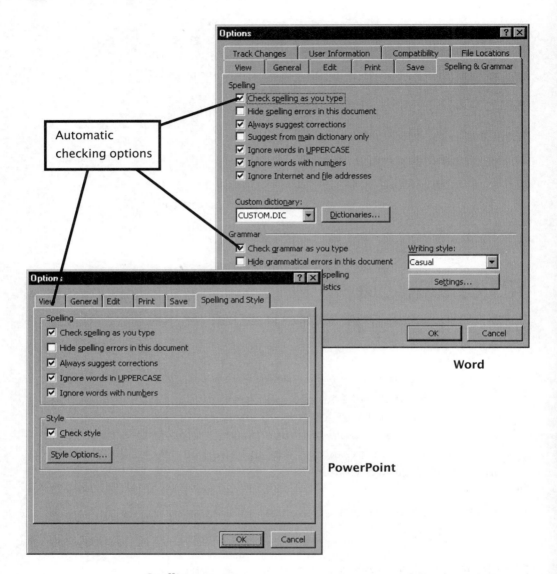

Spelling errors

To find out what Word or PowerPoint suggests as an alternative, right-click on the highlighted word.

- If you wish to change the word in your document to one of those listed, click on the word that you want to use.

- If you choose **Ignore All**, the word will not be highlighted again in the document in this working session.

- If you choose **Add**, the word will be added to the dictionary, and it will be recognised as a correctly-spelt word from now on.

Grammatical errors

These can be dealt with in a similar way. When you right-click on the error, the application will display the problem, and suggest a remedy if it can. You can choose whether you wish to change your text to that suggested or ignore the suggestion.

Checking spelling and grammar when you are ready

You can easily check your spelling and grammar at any time using the **Spelling and Grammar** tool.

Try it: Start checking

① Click the **Spelling and Grammar** tool [ABC] on the Standard toolbar.

The application will spell check your file. Respond to the prompts as you see fit. When the checking is complete, a prompt will appear to tell you so.

② Click **OK** to return to your file.

Key points regarding spelling and grammar checkers

- Spell checkers may not pick up all your errors – if you have a correctly spelt word in the wrong context, the spell checker will not pick it up as an error.

- The options for the spelling and grammar checkers can be found in the **Tools ▶ Options** dialog box.

- The language used by your spell checker is displayed on the Status bar.

- To change the language used, go into **Tools ▶ Language ▶ Set Language** (or double-click the language display on the Status bar).

Always proofread your documents – don't rely on the spelling or grammar checkers finding everything

Formatting

Font formatting

One way of enhancing your text is to apply font formatting to it. Effects can be applied to individual characters in your document.

The most commonly used font formatting options have tools on the Formatting toolbar – other options can be found in the Format, Font dialog box. The formatting toolbar varies a little from application to application – this one is from Word. The formatting options discussed here are available in *all* Office applications.

Try it: Format text

To format text or data as you type it in:

① Switch on the formatting option(s) required.

② Type in text or data.

③ Switch off or change the formatting option.

To apply formatting to (or change the formatting of) existing text or data:

① Select the text or data.

② Switch the option on or off, or apply additional formats.

Try it: Emphasise text

Useful keyboard shortcuts
[Ctrl]-[B] bold
[Ctrl]-[I] italics
[Ctrl]-[U] underline

B   switches bold on or off;

/   switches italic on or off;

U   switches underline on or off.

Font styles, size and colour

The font style, size and colour are also easily changed.

To change the font used:

① Click the drop-down arrow to the right of the **Font** tool on the **Formatting** toolbar.

② Scroll through the list of available fonts until you see the font you want to use.

③ Click on the font.

To change the size of font:

① Click the drop-down arrow to the right of the **Font Size** tool ⌑10⌑ on the **Formatting** toolbar.

② Scroll through the list of available font sizes until you see the size you want to use.

③ Click on it.

To change the colour of font:

① Click the drop-down arrow to the right of the **Font Color** tool on the **Formatting** toolbar to display the **Font Color** toolbar.

② Select the colour you want to use.

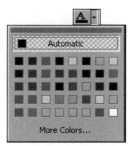

Key points to note on formatting

• You have access to all of the formatting options in an application in the **Format** menu.

Paragraph/cell formatting

The default paragraph (Word/PowerPoint) or cell (Excel/Access) formatting options gives you a left-aligned text, with single-line spacing. If this is not the formatting you require you can change it.

Try it: Alignment

▤	centres a paragraph, or text or data within a cell
▤	justifies a paragraph (or paragraphs)
▤	right aligns a paragraph (or paragraphs)
▤	left aligns a paragraph (or paragraphs)

Useful keyboard shortcuts –

[Ctrl]-[L] left align

[Ctrl]-[R] right align

[Ctrl]-[J] justify

[Ctrl]-[E] centre

Try it: Borders and shading

Borders and shading can be very useful when it comes to emphasising areas in your file.

To place a border around your paragraph(s) or cell(s):

①   Select the paragraph(s) or cell(s).

②   Click the drop-down arrow to the right of the **Borders** tool to display the **Borders** toolbar.

③   Select the border from the options available.

Click **No borders** to remove unwanted existing borders

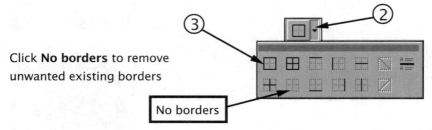

No borders

There are more options in the **Borders and Shading** dialog box. You can apply a border to all four sides (an outside border) using the Box, Shadow or 3-D setting.

①   From the **Format** menu choose **Borders and Shading**...

②   Experiment with the options.

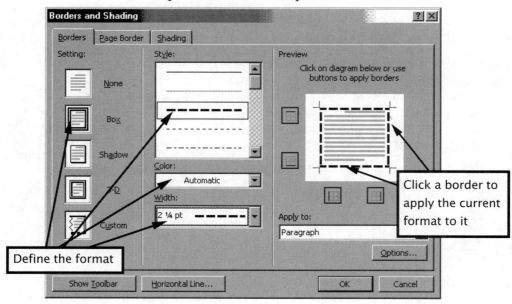

③ Click **OK** or **Cancel** (depending on whether or not you wish to apply the formats you have selected).

You can choose a shading effect for your paragraph(s) or cell(s). Select the **Shading** tab and explore the options.

Click [↶▾] on the Standard toolbar (or press [Ctrl]-[Z]) to Undo an action. Click [↷▾] to Re-do an action

Format Painter

If you need to apply the same formatting to different areas of text or data in your file, you could use the Format Painter to 'paint' the formatting from one area to another.

Try it: Format Painter

① Select some text or data that has been formatted using the options you want to 'paint' onto other text or data.

② Click the **Format Painter** tool [🖌] on the **Standard** toolbar.

③ Click and drag over the text or data you want to 'paint' the formatting onto.

If you want to paint the formats onto several separate pieces of text, double-click on the Format Painter to lock it. When you have finished, click the tool again to unlock it.

Preview and Print

At some stage you will want to print your file. I suggest you *preview* it first to check how it will look. The preview will display a full page of your file on the screen at once (more than one page if you wish) so that you can check how the finished page will look. Basic preview and print options are given here – any that are specific to each application are discussed in the relevant chapters.

Print Preview

• To preview your document, click the **Print Preview** tool [🔍] on the **Standard** toolbar.

A full-page preview of your document will appear on screen and the Print Preview toolbar will be displayed. Click [Close] on the Print Preview toolbar to return to your document window.

To print one copy of your file:

* Click the **Print** tool 🖨 on the **Standard** or **Print Preview** toolbar.

Key point to note on printing

* If you want more than one copy of the current file printed, open the **File** menu and choose **Print**. You can specify that and other options you require in the dialog box.

Drawings

You can easily draw shapes and create images in your files using the Drawing toolbar.

To display the Drawing toolbar:

* Click the **Drawing** tool 🖋 on the **Standard** toolbar.

Or

* Right-click on any toolbar that is displayed, and select **Drawing** from the list of toolbars.

Try it: Drawing

To draw a line, arrow, rectangle or oval:

① Click the line, arrow, rectangle or oval tool ＼ ＼ □ ○ on the **Drawing** toolbar.

② Click and drag where you want to 'draw' your shape.

To draw a square or circle:

① Select the rectangle or oval tool on the **Drawing** toolbar.

② Click (don't drag) to get a 2.5cm square or circle.

Or

② Hold down [Shift] while you drag to create a regular shape to the desired size.

To enter an AutoShape:

① Click the **AutoShapes** tool.

② Pick a category.

③ Select a shape.

④ Click where you want the shape.

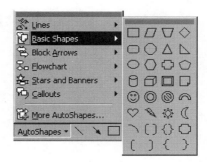

To add a text box:

① Select the **Text Box** tool 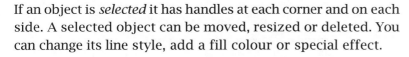.

② Click at the position you want the shape.

③ Type in your text.

If an object is *selected* it has handles at each corner and on each side. A selected object can be moved, resized or deleted. You can change its line style, add a fill colour or special effect.

Formatting shapes

To move a shape	Place mouse pointer within the shape and click and drag
To resize a shape	Place mouse pointer over a handle and click and drag
To delete a shape	Press [Delete]
To change line style	Click the Line Style tool and choose a style
To change line colour	Click the arrow by the Line Color field and pick one
To change the fill colour	Click the arrow by the Fill Color tool and choose a colour
To add a shadow	Click the Shadow tool and select an effect
To add a 3-D effect	Click the 3-D effect tool and choose from the options

Select an object and create special effects on it using these tools

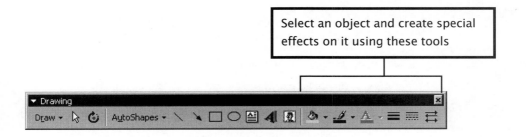

WordArt

WordArt gives you the option of creating special text effects in your file.

Try it: WordArt

① Click the **Insert WordArt** tool on the **Drawing** toolbar.

② Select a **WordArt style** as required from the Gallery.

③ Click **OK**.

You can adjust the size and position of a WordArt object in the same way as a drawing object

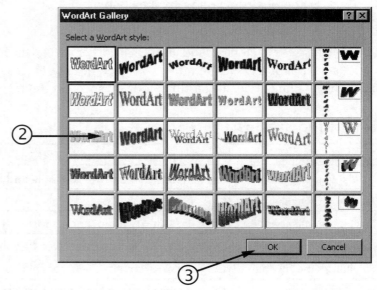

④ At the **Edit WordArt Text** dialog box, enter (and format) the text.

⑤ Click **OK**.

⑥ Adjust the size and shape of your WordArt object as required.

⑦ Reposition your object if necessary.

The WordArt toolbar

• Experiment with the tools to see the effects they produce.

Pictures

If you've installed Microsoft Office you'll find you've access to lots of ClipArt. If you've Internet access, you'll also find lots of clips online.

Try it: Insert ClipArt

① Click the **Insert ClipArt** tool 📷 on the **Drawing** toolbar.

② Select a **Category** in the **Insert ClipArt** dialog box.

③ Scroll through the clips and select the one you want to use (or click under the pictures to display more).

④ Click the **Preview clip** tool to magnify the image if you want a closer look at it.

⑤ Click the **Insert clip** tool to place the image in your document.

⑥ **Close** the Insert ClipArt dialog box.

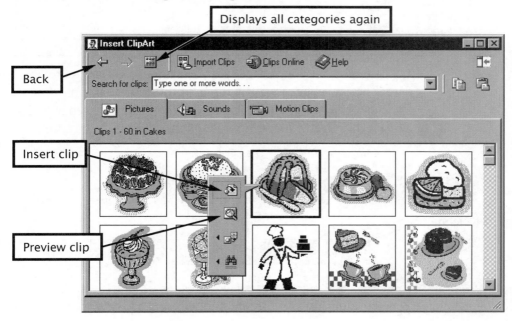

To search for clips:

If you find scrolling through the clips a bit tedious, you can use search for clips that may be suitable.

① Open the **Insert ClipArt** dialog box.

② Enter the keyword you're looking for, e.g. 'violinist', in the search for clips field.

③ Press [**Enter**].

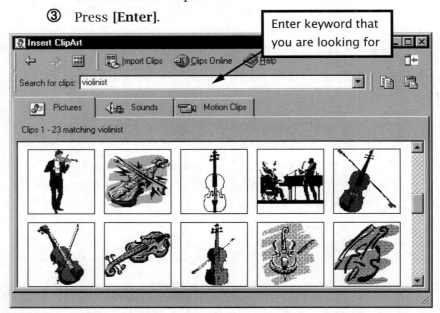

The clips that you insert into your document can be formatted in a number of ways – the best thing to do is experiment. When an inserted clip is selected, the **Picture** toolbar is displayed. You can use the toolbar to modify your picture.

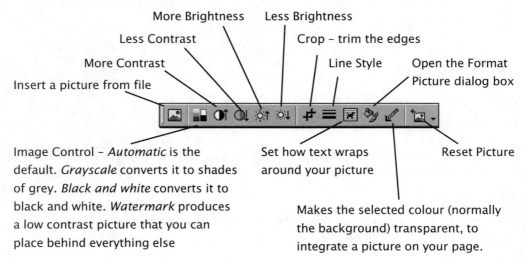

Key points about ClipArt

- The clip you have inserted can be resized, moved or deleted using the same techniques as with drawing objects.

- Double-click on the clip to open the **Format** dialog box to access all the formatting options for the object.

Try it: Crop a clip

① Select the picture.

② Click the **Crop** tool.

③ Drag a resizing handle to crop the bits you don't want.

Try it: Insert from file

If you have a picture on disk that is not in the Gallery (perhaps a photograph you've scanned in), you can still insert it.

① Open the **Insert** menu.

② Select **Picture**.

③ Choose **From File**...

④ Locate the file you want to insert – explore the folders.

⑤ Select the file and click **Insert**.

Toolbars

Sometimes toolbars will appear and disappear automatically. For example, you may have noticed that the Picture toolbar appears when a ClipArt object selected, the WordArt toolbar appears when a WordArt object is selected. You can opt to show or hide toolbars whenever you want.

Provided you have at least one toolbar displayed, you can use the shortcut method to show or hide any toolbar.

Try it: Show and hide toolbars

Using the shortcut menu:

① Right-click on a toolbar.

- Open toolbars have a tick beside their name.

② Click on the toolbar name you wish to show or hide.

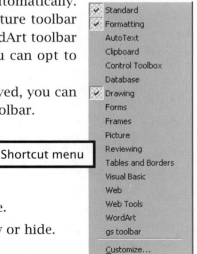

Shortcut menu

If no toolbars are displayed, you must use the **View** menu to show them again.

① Open the **View** menu and choose **Toolbars**.

② Click on the one you want to show.

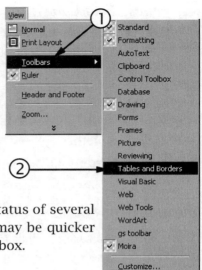

Using either of the methods above, you can show or hide one toolbar at a time. If you want to change the display status of several toolbars at the one time, it may be quicker to use the Customize dialog box.

Moving toolbars

Toolbars can be positioned *anywhere* on your screen. The Standard and Formatting toolbars are normally displayed along the top of your screen.

Toolbars can be docked in one of the four docking areas – at the top, bottom, left and right of your screen. You can also leave your toolbar floating in the work area if you prefer

Try it: Move a toolbar

① If the toolbar is *docked*, point to its left end (if it is docked at the top or bottom of the screen) or top end (if docked at the left or right) – where the two raised lines are.

• If the toolbar is not docked, point to its Title bar.

② Drag and drop the toolbar to the position you want it.

Customising toolbars

There are more tools that give shortcuts to commands than are displayed on the normal toolbars. You can customise your toolbars by adding tools, or by removing those you don't use.

Try it: Add tools to an existing toolbar

① Right-click on the toolbar then click on **Customize**…

② Select the **Commands** tab in the **Customize** dialog box.

③ Select a **Category** from the list and scroll through the **Commands** list to see what tools are available.

④ Drag and drop the command from the **Commands** list onto your toolbar.

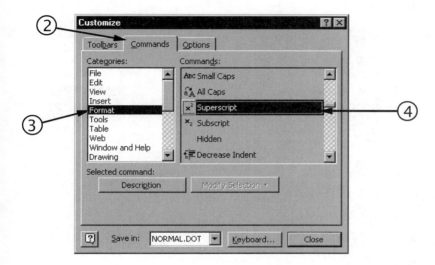

Try it: Remove tools from an existing toolbar

- With the **Customize** dialog box open, drag and drop the tool off the toolbar.

Try it: Move tools on an existing toolbar

- With the **Customize** dialog box open, drag and drop the tool in the position required.

Creating a new toolbar

If you have several commands that you wish to display on a toolbar, but are struggling for room, you should create a new toolbar and add the extra tools to it.

Try it: Create a new toolbar

① At the **Customize** dialog box, select the **Toolbars** tab.

② Click **New**...

③ Give your toolbar a name.

④ Leave the **Make toolbar available to:** *Normal.dot* if you want to be able to use it in all your files.

Move your new toolbar to the position you want it displayed

⑤ Click OK

⑥ Add the tools from the lists on the **Commands** tab.

⑦ Close the **Customize** dialog box when you've finished.

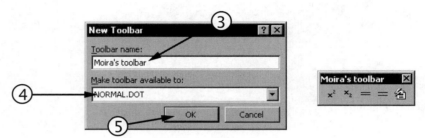

To reset the toolbars back to their original state:

① On the **Toolbars** tab, select the toolbar.

② Click **Reset**...

③ Click **OK**.

⑤ Close the **Customize** dialog box.

You can also show/hide toolbars from here – click on the check box to set or remove the tick

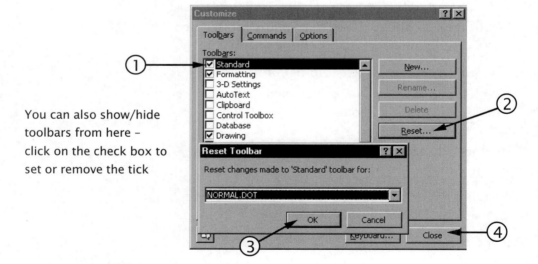

5
Word processing

IN THIS CHAPTER:

- Basic word processing skills
- Font formatting
- Special characters and symbols
- Paragraph formatting
- Preview and Print
- Find and Replace
- View options
- Page Setup
- Tables

Word processing packages are used to produce letters, memos, reports, books, forms, mail shots, etc. This chapter will help you become efficient in the use of your word processor, quickly and easily. The examples have been produced using Word and Works. We discuss basic word processing skills, then go on to consider some effective ways of producing a variety of document layouts.

Getting started

Starting your word processing application

Opening applications – see page 68

If you open Microsoft Word or Works from the Start menu, you will have a new blank document on your screen.

If you are at the Microsoft Works Task Launcher screen you should:

① Select **Programs** in the Task Launcher window.

② Select **Works Word Processor** in the Programs list.

③ Click **Start a blank Word Processor document**.

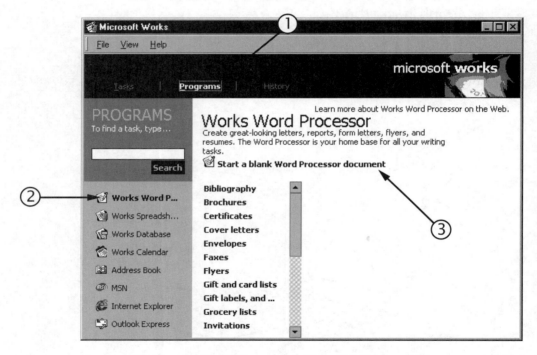

Take a look at the screen. You should be able to recognise:

• Title bar	• Menu bar	• Toolbars
• Minimise	• Maximise/Restore	• Close button
• Border	• Status bar	• Scroll bars
• Rulers	• Document area	

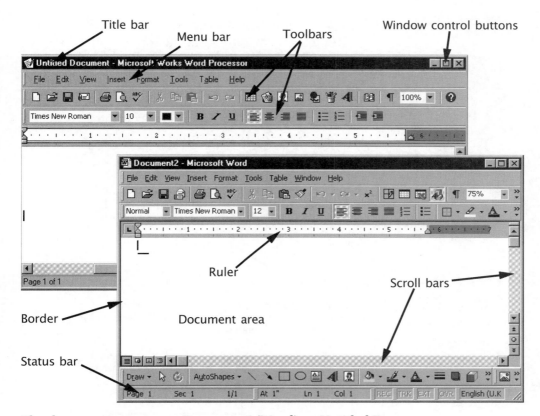

The document name, e.g. *Document1* (Word) or *Untitled Document* (Works), is displayed on the title bar. Each new document you create during a session is given a temporary name following the Document1 or Untitled Document format. When you save your document you should give it a meaningful name instead of the temporary name assigned to it.

Entering text

The insertion point – the flashing black vertical bar – is in the top left of the text area on the first page. You're ready to start – just type!

Key points to remember when entering text

- DO NOT press the [Enter] key at the end of each line. As the text runs onto a new line, the text will automatically wrap at the end of the line.

- DO press the [Enter] key at the end of short lines of text e.g. after lines in an address at the top of a letter or after the last line in a paragraph.

- To leave a clear line between paragraphs, or several empty lines between headings or in the signature block at the end of a letter, press the [Enter] key as often as is necessary to get the effect you want.

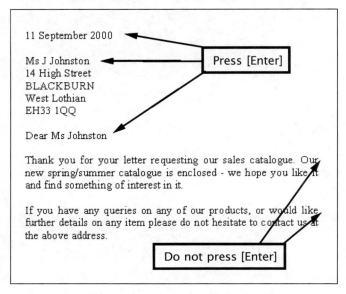

Moving the insertion point

Use the scroll bars to bring the text you want to edit into view if necessary

When you need to fix a mistake, the first thing you have to do is place the insertion point next to the error.

There are several different ways of moving the insertion point. Experiment with the various options as you work.

Using the mouse

① Position the I-beam (the name given to the pointer when it is over a text area) at the place you want to move the insertion point to.

② Click the left mouse button.

Using the keyboard

To move a character or line at a time	←, →, ↑ or ↓
To move right or left a word at a time	[Ctrl] → or ←
To move up or down a paragraph at a time	[Ctrl] ↑ or ↓
To move to the end of the line	[End]
To move to the beginning of the line	[Home]
To move to the beginning of the document	[Ctrl]–[Home]
To move to the end of the document	[Ctrl]–[End]

Editing your text

Try it: Insert new text

① Position the insertion point where you want the new text to appear.

② Type in your new text.

Try it: Delete existing text

① Position the insertion point next to the character that you want to delete.

② To delete characters to the left, press the backspace key ← once for each character.

Or

• To delete characters to the right, press the [Delete] key once for each character.

Both the ← and [Delete] keys repeat – if you hold them down they will zoom through your text removing it much quicker than you could type it in, so be careful with them!

Overtype

You can type over existing text, replacing the old text with the new in one operation, instead of deleting the old then entering the new. Press the [Insert] key to switch Overtype on and off.

• When Overtype mode is on, the text on the Overtype button on the status bar is black.

Hold the [Shift] key down while using the keyboard methods to move the insertion point -- your text will be selected

The [Insert] key switches overtype on and off

Try it: Overtype

Experiment!
You could type:

- a letter to a friend
- notes on a hobby
- a best-seller!

① Switch on *Overtype* mode – press **[Insert]**.

② Position the insertion point within some text and type – the existing text will be replaced with the new text.

③ Switch *Overtype* mode off again – press **[Insert]**.

To insert a new paragraph:

- Position the insertion point where the paragraph break should be and press [Enter] twice if you want to leave a blank line.

To join two paragraphs:

- Move to the end of the upper (or start of the lower paragraph) and delete the space between them.

Key points to note when editing text

- Make sure the insertion point is in the correct place.
- Remember that both the ← and [Delete] are repeat keys.
- The [Insert] key toggles Overtype mode.

Page breaks

As you type in your text a page break will be inserted automatically when you reach the end of the page. However, there may be times when you want a page break to occur at a specific place in your document e.g. at the end of a topic. On such occasions, you can easily insert a manual page break.

With these simple word processing skills, you can produce plain text documents – though the layout might not be very exciting!

Try it: Insert a manual page break

① Position the insertion point where you want a page break.

② Press **[Ctrl]-[Enter]**.

You can delete the manual page break as you would any other character (you can display the manual page break by showing the non-printing characters to make this easier).

Show/Hide non-printing characters

Non-printing characters are the codes that are inserted when you press the spacebar, [Enter], [Tab] or manual page break.

These characters control the layout of your document, but don't print – hence they are *non-printing*.

- You can toggle the display of your non-printing characters at any time by clicking the Show/Hide tool ¶.

If you display your non-printing characters, the symbols are:

¶ [Enter] → [Tab] • [Space]

Font formatting

The commonly used formatting options are on the Formatting toolbar. You should also explore the Font dialog box in your application to see what other options are available.

Try it: Formatting using options in the Font dialog box

① Open the **Format menu** and choose **Font**.

② Choose the effects you want – a preview is displayed in the **Preview** or **Sample** panel (explore the **Font**, **Character Spacing** and **Text Effects** tabs in Word).

③ Click **OK** to apply the effects to your text, or **Cancel** to return to your document without making any changes.

Standard formatting routines are used when formatting text – you can select a format option then type, or type your text, then select it and apply the format

Formatting options that are fairly standard across the applications were discussed in Chapter 4

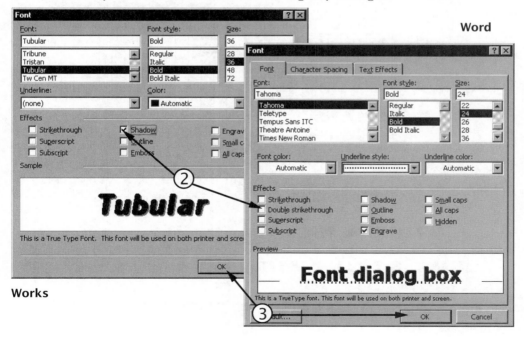

Word

Works

Special characters and symbols

Useful keyboard
shortcuts for
special symbols:
[Alt]-[Ctrl]-[C] ©
[Alt]-[Ctrl]-[T] ™
[Alt]-[Ctrl]-[R] ®
Check out the
**Insert Special
Character** dialog
box in Works or
the **Symbol** dialog
box in Word for a
full list

Most of the characters that you will want to type into your document are available through the keyboard. However, there may be times when you want a special character that is not there. You may find the character in the Symbol dialog box.

Try it: Insert a symbol

① Place the insertion point where you want the character.

② Open the **Insert** menu.

③ Choose **Symbol** (Word) or **Special Character** (Works).

④ Select the font to choose a character from (you'll need to spend some time exploring your fonts).

⑤ Select a character – click on it.

⑥ Click **Insert**.

⑦ Click **Close** to close the dialog box.

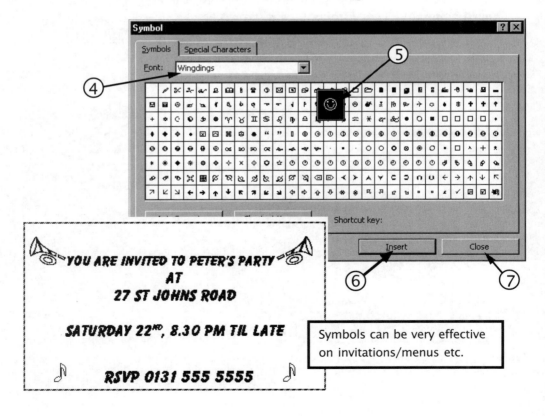

Symbols can be very effective on invitations/menus etc.

Paragraph formatting

Some formatting options are applied to complete paragraphs, regardless of whether the paragraph consists of a few words or several lines.

A paragraph is created each time you press the [Enter] key

Paragraph formatting options include:

- Alignment (Chapter 4) • Line spacing • Indents
- Borders and Shading (Chapter 4) • Tabs
- Bulleted /Numbered lists

Line spacing

Initially, your line spacing is set to single. You can easily change to double or 1½ line spacing if you wish.

You can set the line spacing with the keyboard shortcuts.

If the text is already typed in, remember to select the paragraph(s) first

Try it: Change the line spacing

- Double line spacing   [Ctrl]-[2]
- 1½ line spacing   [Ctrl]-[5]
- Single line spacing   [Ctrl]-[1]

You could also open the **Format ▶ Paragraph** dialog box and set the line spacing from there.

Bulleted and numbered lists

You can easily add bullets or numbers automatically to your paragraphs.

Try it: Switch bullets and numbering on and off

① Click the **Bullets** tool to switch bullets on or the **Numbering** tool to switch numbering on.

Bullets and numbering are toggles – click the tool to switch them on and off

② Type in your paragraphs, pressing **[Enter]** at the end of each one.

③ Press **[Enter]** twice at the end of your list to cancel the bullets or numbering.

You can change the bullet or number style from the dialog box.

If you are using Word, at the **Bulleted** tab choose **Customize**, then **Font**, to get access to all the symbols – you can use any of them as bullet characters

Try it: Change the bullet or number style

① Select the paragraphs you want bulleted or numbered.

② Open the **Format** menu and choose **Bullets and Numbering**.

③ Select the **Bulleted** or **Numbered** tab in the dialog box.

④ Choose a bullet or numbering option.

⑤ Click **OK**.

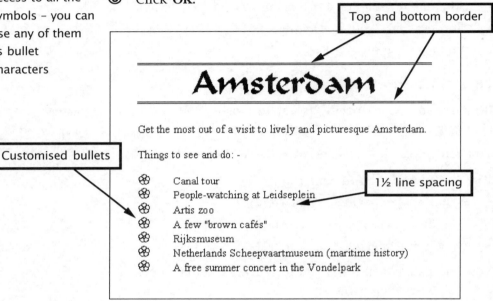

Top and bottom border

Amsterdam

Get the most out of a visit to lively and picturesque Amsterdam.

Things to see and do: -

Customised bullets

1½ line spacing

⊗ Canal tour
⊗ People-watching at Leidseplein
⊗ Artis zoo
⊗ A few "brown cafés"
⊗ Rijksmuseum
⊗ Netherlands Scheepvaartmuseum (maritime history)
⊗ A free summer concert in the Vondelpark

Indents

Useful keyboard shortcuts
[Ctrl]-[M] increases the left indent
[Shift]-[Ctrl]-[M] decreases the left indent of all lines in a paragraph

Your paragraphs normally run the full width of your typing line – from the left margin to the right margin. As you enter your text, it extends along the line until it reaches the right margin and then it automatically wraps to the next line (unless you press the [Enter] key).

You can easily change the amount of the indent between the margin and your text – a useful effect if you want to make a paragraph or two stand out.

Try it: Change the left indent of all lines in a paragraph

① Select the paragraph(s) then:

② Click the **Increase Indent** tool ▨ on the **Formatting** toolbar.

Or

- Click the **Decrease Indent** tool ▣.

Indent markers

You can also use the ruler to set your indents. The ruler must be displayed along the top of your text area.

The indent markers are the two triangles and the small rectangle below them at the left edge of the ruler, and the small triangle at the right.

In Word, open the View menu and choose Ruler to switch the ruler display on and off

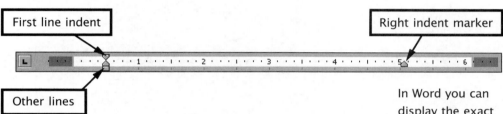

First line indent

Right indent marker

Other lines

In Word you can display the exact position of your indent on the ruler as you drag it – just hold down the [Alt] key while you drag

Try it: Change the indents using the horizontal ruler

Place the insertion point inside the paragraph you want to indent.

To adjust the indent of:

- the first line in the paragraph from the left margin, drag the top triangle at the left edge of the ruler;

- all other lines (except the first) from the left margin, drag the bottom triangle at the left edge;

- all lines in the paragraph from the left margin, drag the rectangle below the two triangles at the left;

- all lines in the paragraph from the right margin, drag the triangle at the right edge of the ruler.

To set the indent you require:

- Drag the appropriate indent marker along the ruler to the required position.

Examples of Indents

This paragraph has had the first line indented from the left margin. All other lines in the paragraph go back to the left margin.

In this paragraph the first line is at the left margin, but all other lines have been indented. This type of indent is called a "hanging" indent.

All lines in this paragraph have been indented from the left and the right margin.

This paragraph is running from the left to right margin and is the default paragraph formatting for your text.

To adjust the indent of several paragraphs at the same time, select them first

You can also adjust the indents from the **Paragraph** dialog box if you prefer.

① Open the **Format** menu and choose **Paragraph**.

② Set the **Left**, **Right** and/or **First line** indents as required.

③ Click **OK**.

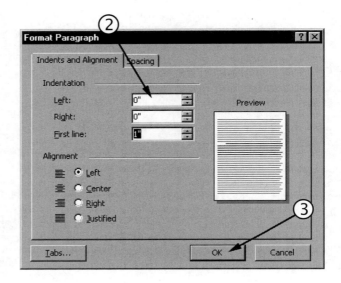

Tabs

Tabs are used to align your text horizontally on the typing line. If you want to type up a list of names and telephone numbers you can use tabs to align each column.

The default tabs are set every half inch along the ruler – the small dark grey marks along the bottom edge of the ruler indicate their positions.

Each time you press the [Tab] key on your keyboard the insertion point jumps forward to the next tab position that is set. The default tabs have left alignment – when you enter your text or numbers the left edge of the text or data entered is at the tab position.

Tabs can be aligned to the left, right or centre, or to a decimal or bar character.

Alignment	Effect	Possible use
Left	The left edge is at tab	Any text or numbers
Right	The right edge is at tab	Text, or numbers you want to line up on the unit
Centre	Centred under the tab	Anything
Decimal	Decimal point under tab	Figures that you want to line up on the decimal point

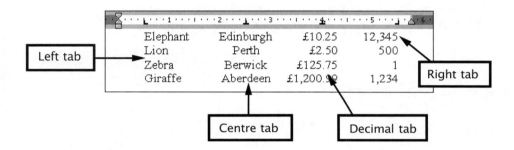

If you need to use tabs and the pre-set ones are not what you require, you must set tabs at the positions you need them.

Try it: Work with tabs using the ruler

To set a tab:

① Select the type of tab required – click the Style button to the left of the ruler until you've got the alignment option required (Word only).

Right-click on the ruler in Works to set a right tab

Left ☐   Centre ☐   Right ☐   Decimal ☐

② Point to the lower half of the ruler and click – your tab is set (a left tab will be set in Works).

To move a tab:

•   Drag it along the ruler to its correct position.

To delete a tab:

•   Drag it down off the ruler, and drop it.

To set tabs in the Tabs dialog box:

If you need to
move, delete or
set a tab for
several
paragraphs that
you have already
typed, remember
to select the
paragraphs first

① Open the **Format** menu and choose **Tabs**.

② Enter the **Tab stop position** (the distance the tab will be from the margin).

③ Select the alignment required.

④ Set a leader character (if required).

⑤ Click **Set**.

⑥ Repeat until all your tabs are set.

⑦ Click **OK**.

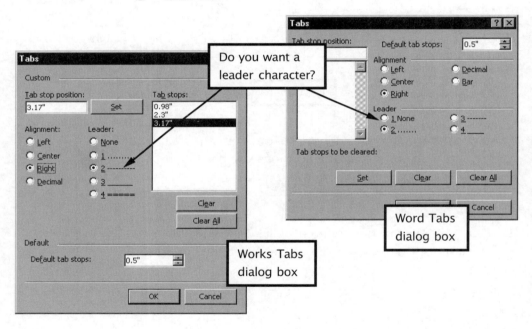

Do you want a leader character?

Word Tabs dialog box

Works Tabs dialog box

EXperiment

Print preview and print

When you preview your file a full page is displayed at a time. You can zoom in and out so that you can read the text.

Preview your file before printing – you can then check that it is displayed effectively on the page

Zoom

If you move the pointer over your page in Print Preview, you will notice it looks like a magnifying glass with a + on it.

*   With the mouse pointer over your page, click the left mouse button to zoom in and out.

Print

*   Click the **Print** tool on the Print Preview toolbar. One copy of the document will be printed.

Print Preview toolbar

The Print Preview window has its own toolbar which can be used to control the display of your document on the screen. The toolbars in Word and Works are very similar – if you point at a tool with the mouse, a Tooltip will tell you what the tool does. Experiment with the tools to see what effect they have.

Word toolbar

Works toolbar

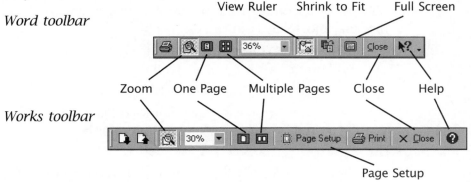

One Page: Click this tool to display your document on the screen one page at a time.

Multiple Pages: In Word, this drops down a grid that you can click and drag over to indicate the number of pages to display at a time. In Works it displays two at a time.

Zoom: Sets the percentage of magnification of the document.

View Ruler (Word): Toggles the display of the vertical and horizontal rulers.

Shrink to Fit (Word): If a small amount of text appears on the last page of your document you may be able to reduce the number of pages by clicking this tool. Word decreases the size of each font used in the document to get the text to fit on to one page less.

Page Setup (Works): Displays the Page Setup dialog box.

Full Screen (Word): You can remove most of the toolbars, menu bar, etc. to get a 'clean screen' display. To return the screen to normal, click **Close Full Screen** on the **Full Screen** toolbar or press [Esc].

Close: Exits Print Preview and returns you to your document.

Help: In Word this is context sensitive – click the **Help** tool, then click on a toolbar tool, ruler or other screen object to get a brief description of its function. In Works the **Help** tool opens the **Help** panel.

Moving through your document in Print Preview

If you have more than one page in your document, you may want to scroll through the pages in Print Preview to check that they look okay. You can do this by:

*   Clicking the arrow up or arrow down button at the top and bottom of the vertical scroll bar;

Or

*   Clicking the **Previous Page** or **Next Page** button at the bottom of the vertical scroll bar (Word);

Or

*   Clicking the **Next** or **Previous** tools on the Print Preview toolbar (Works).

Print

If you don't just want to print a single copy of your whole file, use the **Print** dialog box.

① Open the **File** menu and choose **Print**.

② Select the **Page range** - *All*, *Current page* (Word), *Pages*, e.g.1,2,4-7,12 (Word) or *From* and *To* (Works).

③ Set the **Number of copies** required – usually 1.

④ Click **OK**.

In Word, if you select some text before opening the Print dialog box, the **Selection** option becomes active so that you can print out just the selected text

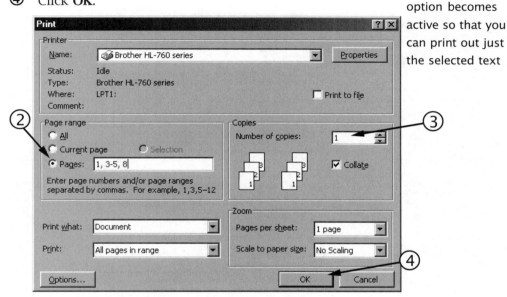

Find and Replace

If you're working on a longer document and want to find some text that you know you've typed in, you could use the Find command to help you find it (rather than scroll through the pages looking for it).

Try it: Find some text

① Open the **Edit** menu and choose **Find...**

② Enter the text you want to find in the **Find what:** field.

③ Complete the other search options as required – these can be toggled by clicking the **Less/More button** (Word).

④ Click **Find Next**.

[Ctrl]-[F] displays the Find tab; [Ctrl]-[H] displays the Replace tab

- The first occurrence of the text will be highlighted. If necessary, click **Find Next** to move on to the next occurrence.

⑤ When the appropriate text has been located, click **Cancel** to return to your document.

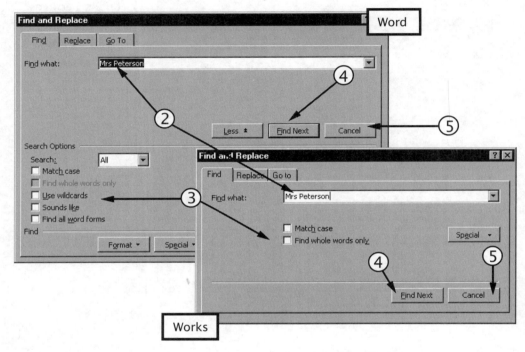

Try it: Replace some text

To do a selective replacement, click **Find Next** to locate the text. If you want to replace that occurrence click **Replace**, it not, click **Find Next** again to move on to the next occurrence

If you've typed something incorrectly several times, e.g. you typed 'Mr Donaldson' when it should have been 'Mrs Peterson' use the Replace feature to fix it.

① Open the **Edit** menu and choose **Replace...**

② Complete the **Replace** tab with details of the text you want to find and replace in the **Find what:** and **Replace with:** fields.

③ Select any other options required.

④ Click **Find Next**.

- The first occurrence of the text will be highlighted.

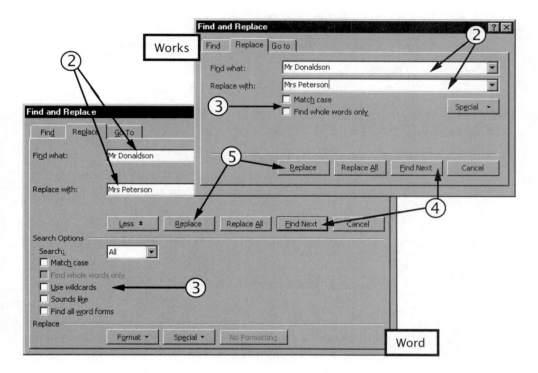

⑤ Click **Replace** to replace this one occurrence, then click **Find Next** again;

Or

• Click **Replace All** to replace all occurrences automatically.

View options in Word

When working in a document, there are several view options. The view option controls how your document looks on the screen – not how it will print out. You usually work in Normal view or Print Layout view when entering and editing text.

Normal View

Normal View is the default view for working in Word. It is the view usually used for entering, editing and formatting text.

The page layout is simplified in Normal View – margins, headers and footers, multiple columns, etc. – are not displayed.

View tools

⊞ ◪ ▣ ▤ , from left to right, Normal, Web Layout, Print Layout and Outline

Try it: Change to Normal view

- Open the **View** menu and choose **Normal**.

Or

- Click the **Normal view** tool at the bottom left of the screen.

Print Layout view

In this view the margins (and any headers or footers you have within them), pictures, drawings, multiple columns, etc. are all displayed in their true position on the page.

Try it: Change to Page Layout view

- Open the **View** menu and choose **Print Layout**.

Or

- Click the **Print Layout View** tool.

Zoom

You can also change the zoom (magnification) options when viewing your document. Click the drop-down arrow at the Zoom tool `85%` ▾ on the Standard toolbar and select the option required from the list.

Page Setup

You can change the margins, orientation, paper size and header and footer options in the Page Setup dialog box.

Margins

Measurements can be in inches, cm, mm, points or picas. The unit can be set in the **Tools, Options** dialog box – select the General tab in Word

Margins are the white space between the edge of the page and your text. The default settings for the standard A4 size paper are a top and bottom margin of 1" and a left and right margin of 1.25". You can change the margins if you wish.

Try it: to change the margin setting

① Open the **File menu** and choose **Page Setup...**

② Select the **Margins** tab.

③ Edit the margin fields as required.

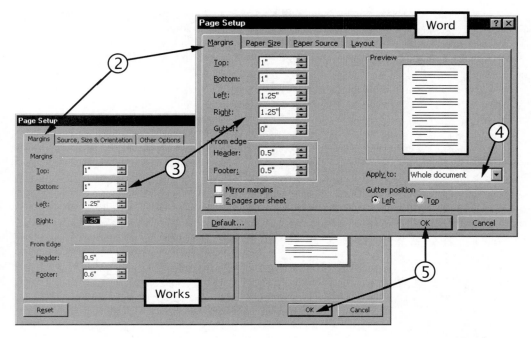

④ Specify the area of your document you want to apply the changes to in the **Apply to:** field – *Whole document, This point forward* or *This section* (Word only, if the document has more than one section).

⑤ Click **OK**.

Orientation and Paper Size

The orientation of a page can be portrait (tall) or landscape (wide). The default orientation is portrait. You can change the orientation of your pages for all of your document or for part of it as required.

Try it: Change the orientation and/or paper size

① Open the **File** menu and choose **Page Setup...**

② Select the **Paper Size** tab (Word) or **Source, Size & Orientation** tab (Works).

③ Choose the **Orientation** required.

④ Set the **Paper Size** required.

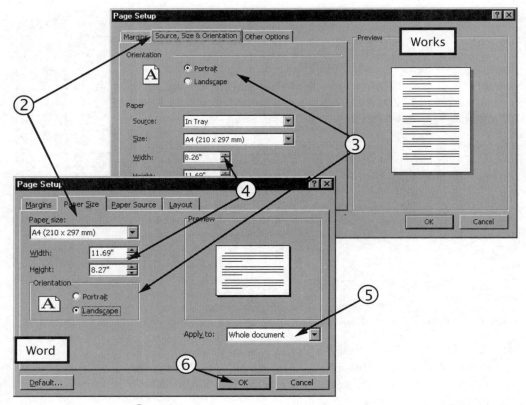

⑤ Specify the area of your document you want to apply the changes to in the **Apply to:** field.

⑥ Click **OK**.

Headers/footers

Headers and footers are displayed at the top and bottom of each page in your document. They usually contain things like page numbers, the name of the author of the document, the filename or the date that the document was produced.

Experiment with the header and footer options in your application.

To insert a header or footer:

① Open the **View** menu.

② Choose **Header and Footer**.

Newsletter   January 2001

FOR SALE

····
Set of new golf clubs.
Unwanted gift, never
used. Any reasonable
offer considered.
Tel: 222 0000
····

Kittens
Free to good home.
Tel: Jill on 330 1000

Yamaha Tenor Saxophone.
Excellent condition.
Complaints from
neighbours forces sale!

£500 ono
Tel: Pete on 200 2000

Page 3

Key points on the header and footer areas

- The insertion point moves to the header area and the Header and Footer toolbar is displayed.

- The main document text is dimmed.

- The header and footer areas have a centre tab set in the middle of the line and a right tab at the end.

You can type any text you wish into the header and footer areas. Use the tabs to help you position the insertion point as necessary. You can format your text in the same way as you format text in the main document area.

The Header and Footer toolbar is displayed – use its tools to insert fields that will be completed and updated automatically by Word or Works.

Use the **Show Previous** and **Show Next** tools to move between the headers and footers when you are in the header and footer areas in Word

Word header/footer toolbar

Header and footer tools (from left to right)

Insert AutoText	Insert filename, author name, etc.
Page Number	Inserts automatic page numbering
Total Number of Pages	Inserts the total number of pages in the document
Format Page Number	Choose alternative formats for your page numbers
Insert Date	Inserts the date that the document is printed
Insert Time	Inserts the time that the document is printed
Page Setup	Displays the dialog box so you can set up header and footer options
Show/Hide document text	Toggles the display of the document text
Same as Previous	Makes/breaks link between headers and footers in different sections of a document
Switch between Header and Footer	Switches between the header and footer area
Show Previous	Displays the next header or footer in document (if document divided into sections)
Show Next	Displays the previous header or footer in document (if document divided into sections)
Close	Returns you to your document

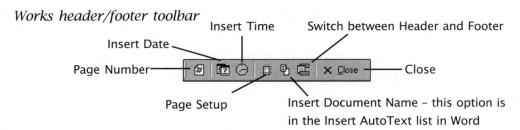

Works header/footer toolbar

Insert Date

Insert Time

Switch between Header and Footer

Page Number — Close

Page Setup

Insert Document Name – this option is in the Insert AutoText list in Word

Header and footer options

Header and footer options are specified in the Page Setup dialog box. The headers and footers themselves are set up through View, Headers and Footers (discussed above). You can have the same header and footer on every page of your document or you could switch them off for the first page, or have different ones on odd and even pages (Word only).

Try it: Set header and footer options

① Open the **File** menu and choose **Page Setup**...

Or

• If you are in Headers and Footers View, click **Page Setup**.

② Select the **Layout** tab (Word) or **Other Options** tab (Works).

③ Set the Header and Footer options.

④ Specify the area in the **Apply to:** field (Word only).

⑤ Click **OK**.

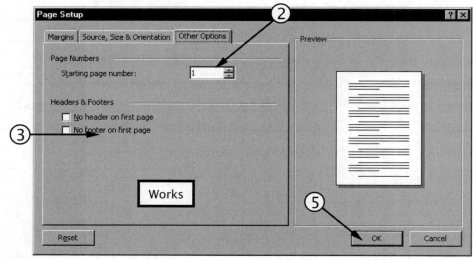

Try it: Set different headers and footers within a document (Word)

① Open the **File menu** and choose **Page Setup...**

② Select the **Layout** tab.

③ Select the checkboxes as required on the **Layout** tab.

④ Click **OK.**

You can have different headers and footers on the first page of a document, or on odd and even pages, or different headers and footers in each section (in Word)

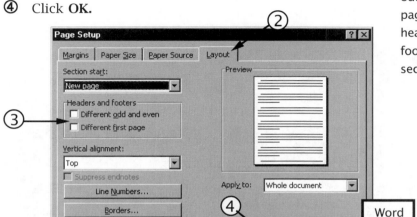

Tables

Tables are used to help you arrange text and data in columns on your page.

Key points in tables

* Tables consist of rows and columns.
* Where a row and column intersect is known as a cell.
* Press the [Tab] key to move forward to the next cell.
* Hold the [Shift] key down and press [Tab] to move back to the previous cell.

Or

* Click in the cell you want to move to.

		Cell	

Try it: Create a table

① Place the insertion point where you want the table to go.

② Click the **Insert Table** tool ▦ on the **Standard** toolbar.

In Word

③ Click and drag over the grid that appears until you get the number of rows and columns required, then release the mouse button – you have an empty table.

In Works:

④ Specify the options in the dialog box.

⑤ Click **OK**.

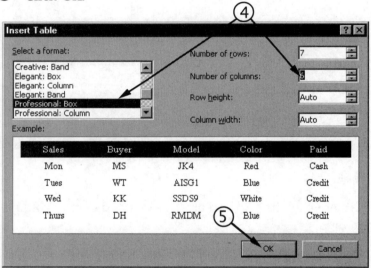

Key points about selecting cells in a table

To select a group of adjacent cells:

• Click and drag over the cells you want to select.

Or

① Click in the corner cell of the range you want to select.

② Point to the cell in the diagonally opposite corner.

③ Hold the **[Shift]** key down and click.

To select a column:

• Click the top gridline or border of the column (you should get a black arrow pointing downwards).

To select several adjacent columns:
- Click and drag along the top border.

To select a row:
- Click to the left of the row you want to select.
- To select several adjacent rows, click and drag up or down the row selector area (to the left of the table).

To select a cell:
 Click just inside the left edge of the cell.

Key points on working with tables
- When entering text into a cell, you will find that the text automatically wraps once it reaches the right edge of the cell, and the row deepens to accommodate it (provided you have spaces between the words or press [Enter]).
- If you press [Tab] when the insertion point is in the last cell in the last row of your table, a new row is created.
- You can format your cells, or text within the cells, using the normal formatting options, e.g. bold, colour, size, alignment (within the cell), borders and shading, etc.

Column width

In most cases, you won't want all your columns to be the same width – it depends what you're entering into them. You can easily change the column width. There are several methods you might like to try – use whatever you find easiest. The insertion point must be within a table when using these.

AutoFit (Word)

You must have some text or data in your columns to give AutoFit something to work on.

- Double-click the border or gridline to the right of the column whose width you want to change.

You will also find a number of AutoFit options in the Table menu. Experiment with them to see how they work.

Manual adjustment

① Position the mouse pointer over the gridline or border to the right of the column you want to adjust.

② Click and drag the border or gridline as required.

Or

③ Click and drag the **Move Table Column** marker (on the ruler) which is above the right border of the column you want to adjust.

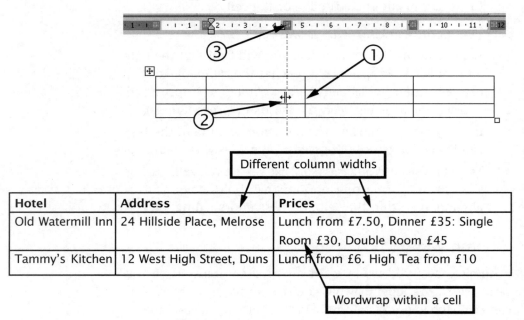

Different column widths

Hotel	Address	Prices
Old Watermill Inn	24 Hillside Place, Melrose	Lunch from £7.50, Dinner £35: Single Room £30, Double Room £45
Tammy's Kitchen	12 West High Street, Duns	Lunch from £6. High Tea from £10

Wordwrap within a cell

Insert and delete rows and columns

When working with your table, you may find that you need to insert (or delete) rows or columns.

To insert a row or column (Word):

① Select the row that will be below the new row, or the column that will go to the right of the new one.

② Right-click on the selected area.

③ Choose **Insert Rows** or **Insert Columns** from the shortcut menu.

To insert a row or column (Works):

① Place the insertion point inside the row or column that will go next to the one you are going to insert.

② Open the **Table** menu.

③ Choose **Insert Row** or **Insert Column**.

④ Select either **Before Current Row/Column** or **After Current Row/Column** as required.

You may find that you have to adjust the width of your columns to accommodate the new columns you add.

Tables are great! Use them for lists, forms, calendars (here's mine!), etc. Experiment lots with them!

To delete a row or column:

① Select the row or column.

② Right-click on the selected area.

③ Select **Delete Rows** or **Delete Columns** (the choice depends on what you selected at step 1).

To delete an entire table (Word):

① Place the insertion point anywhere in the table.

② Open the **Table menu** and choose **Delete**.

③ Click **Table**.

To delete an entire table (Works):

① Place the insertion point anywhere inside the table.

② Open the **Table** menu and choose **Select Table**.

③ Open the **Table** menu and choose **Delete Table**.

• If you select some cells in your table then press [Delete], the contents are deleted, but the table remains in place.

Table Autoformat

You can of course format the text, data and cells within your table using the formatting toolbar and the dialog boxes. (In Works, you can select the format required when you create your table.)

There are also several table *Autoformats* that you can use to quickly format your table.

① Click anywhere inside your table.

② Open the **Table** menu and choose **Table Autoformat** (Word) **or Table Format** (Works).

③ Select an **Autoformat/Format** from the dialog box.

④ Select or deselect the checkboxes as required until you have the formatting options required (Word only).

⑤ Click **OK**.

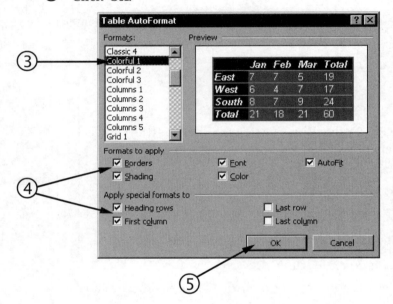

6
Spreadsheets

IN THIS CHAPTER:

- Starting a spreadsheet
- Spreadsheet jargon
- Entering and editing data
- Formatting options
- Formulas and functions
- Sort
- Charts
- Preview, Page Layout and Print

If you have figures to analyse, budgets to manage, or forecasts to project – then spreadsheets are just what you're looking for. This chapter introduces some of the features that you would expect to find in any spreadsheet package. The examples are from Excel and Works – but other spreadsheets will have similar capabilities. This is a doing chapter, so have a read, switch on your computer, and have a go!

Starting a spreadsheet

If you open Microsoft Excel or Microsoft Works through the Start menu (as discussed in Chapter 4), you will have a new blank spreadsheet on your screen.

If you are at the Microsoft Works Task Launcher screen you should:

① Select **Programs** in the **Task Launcher** window.

② Select **Works Spreadsheet** in the programs list.

③ Click **Start a blank Spreadsheet**.

Take a look at the screen.

You should be able to recognise:

- Title Bar
- Menu Bar
- Toolbars
- Minimise
- Maximise/Restore
- Close button
- Border
- Status Bar
- Scroll bars
- Worksheet area

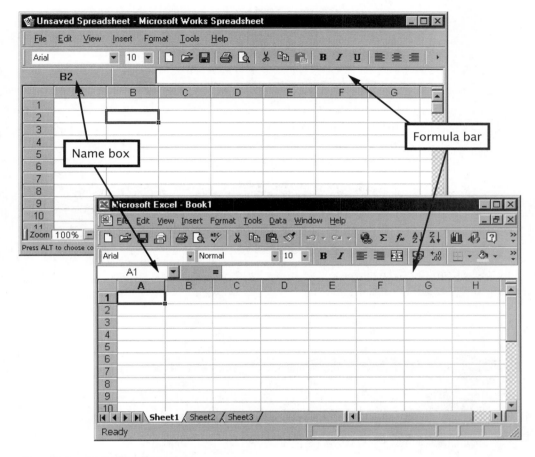

Spreadsheet jargon

Before going any further, spend a little time getting familiar with some of the jargon you will encounter. There's nothing difficult about it – once you know what it means!

Spreadsheet, workbooks and worksheets

In Works your file is called a **spreadsheet**. Each file consists of one **worksheet** or page.

In Excel, the files that you create are called **workbooks**. Each workbook consists of a number of **worksheets** (the default number is three). You can add more worksheets to an Excel workbook if necessary, or remove any that you don't

In Excel, a workbook consists of a number of worksheets

need. Related data is usually best kept on separate worksheets within the same workbook – this makes it easier for you to find and manage your data.

Rows, columns and cells

The worksheet area consists of rows, columns and cells. Rows are identified by the numbers displayed down the left side of the worksheet area. There are lots of rows on a worksheet - 16,384 in Works and 65,536 in Excel!

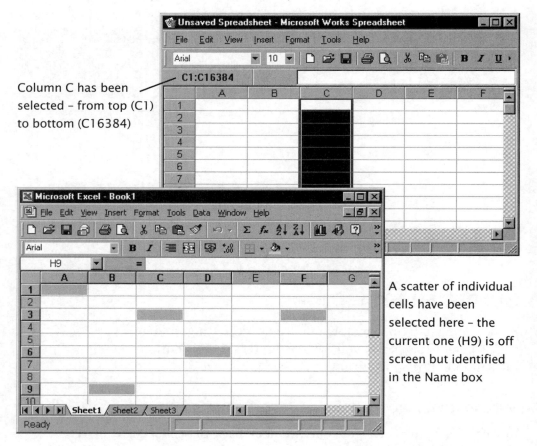

Column C has been selected – from top (C1) to bottom (C16384)

A scatter of individual cells have been selected here – the current one (H9) is off screen but identified in the Name box

Columns are identified by letters displayed along the top of the worksheet. Column C is highlighted in the top illustration. The columns are labelled A to Z, then, after Z, columns are labelled AA to AZ, then BA to BZ, and so on to IV, giving 256 columns in all!

Where a row and column intersect you have a cell. Each of the rectangular areas on your worksheet is a cell. Cells are identified using a cell name or address. A cell address consists of the column letter followed by the row number of the column and row that intersect to create the cell.

Cells A1, B9, C3, D6 and F3 have been highlighted in this screenshot.

You can use spreadsheets to manage budgets, analyse your stocks and shares, keep tabs on your finances, etc.

Key points: text, data, formulas and functions

The cells in your worksheet will eventually contain text, numeric data, formulas or functions.

*   Text is used for titles or narrative to describe the figures you are presenting – worksheet headings, column headings and row labels will usually be text entries.

*   Numeric data means the figures in your worksheet. The data may be entered through the keyboard, or it may be generated as the result of a calculation.

*   Formulas are used to perform calculations on the numeric data in your worksheet. Formulas are used to add the value in one cell to that in another or multiply the values in different cells, etc. Some of your formulas will be very basic while others may be quite complex.

*   Functions are predefined formulas that perform simple or complex calculations on your data. There are many different kinds of functions set up in Excel – statistical, logical, financial, database, engineering, and many more. You're bound to find some useful ones, whatever type of data you work with.

Key points – moving around your worksheet

Before you can enter anything into a cell, you must make the cell you want to work on active (or current). To make a single cell active, you must select it. You can easily move onto any cell (thus making it active) using either the keyboard or the mouse.

The active cell has a dark border. The address of the active cell appears in the Name Box to the left of the Formula bar.

To make a cell the active cell	Scroll the cell into view if necessary, and click
To go to the next cell	Use the ←,→, ↓ and ↑ arrows on keyboard
To go to the cell directly below the current one	Press [Enter]
To go to a specific cell address	1. Press the **[F5]** key 2. Enter the address of the cell in the **Reference** field of the **Go To** dialog box and click **OK**
To go to Cell A1	[Ctrl]-[Home]
To go to the end of your work area	[Ctrl]-[End]

Entering and editing data

Entering text or data into your worksheet is easy.

Try it: Enter text and data

① Select (make active) the cell you want to enter text or data into.

② Type in the text or data – it will appear in the Formula bar as well as in the active cell.

③ Press **[Enter]** or click the 'tick' button to the left of the Formula bar when you've completed the cell.

Key points to note when entering text

• Text that doesn't fit into a single cell will 'spill over' into the cell to the right if the cell to the right is empty.

• Text that doesn't fit into a single cell will only have the text that fits displayed if the cell to the right is not empty. You may need to widen the column or reduce the font size to display all of the text.

• Text automatically aligns to the left of a cell.

Key points to note when entering numeric data

• If a cell displays '########' instead of figures you will need to change the number format or adjust the column width to show all the data.

• Numeric data automatically aligns to the right of a cell.

Text spills over into empty cells

	A	B	C	D	E	F	G	H	I
1	Lottery Number Tally Sheet								
2									
3	Date	1st	2nd	3rd	4th	5th	6th	Bonus	Win
4	Sat 2 September 00	3	6	12	29	36	46		£0.00
5		2	9	12	25	26	49		£1
6		15	16	33	35	41	45		£
7	Numbers Drawn	3	9	25	30	42	49	22	
8	**Total Won**								£10.00
9	Date	1st	2nd	3rd	4th	5th	6th	Bonus	Win
10	Sat 9 September 00	3	6	12	29	36	46		£0.00
11		2	9	12	25	26	49		£0.00
12		15	16	33	35	41	45		£0.00
13	Numbers Drawn	4	12	22	32	33	45	10	
14	**Total Won**								£0.00

Data aligns to the right

Text left aligns

If you make an error when entering your work, you can fix things by:

* deleting the contents of the cell;
* replacing the contents of the cell;
* editing the contents or the cell.

Try it: Edit your cells

To delete the contents of a cell (or cells):

① Select the cell (or cells) whose contents you want to erase.

② Press the **[Delete]** key on your keyboard.

To replace the contents of a cell:

① Select the cell whose contents you want to replace.

② Type in the text or data that should be in the cell.

To edit the contents of a cell:

① Select the cell whose contents you want to edit.

② Click into the Formula bar and position the insertion point where editing is to take place.

③ Edit the cell contents as required.

④ Press **[Enter]** on your keyboard when you finish editing.

Or

If you change your mind when entering data, and want to cancel what you're doing, press **[Esc]** or click the ☒ to the left of the Formula bar

① Select the cell whose contents you want to edit.

② Press **[F2]**.

③ Edit the cell contents as required.

④ Press **[Enter]** when you have finished editing.

You can edit in the Formula bar or in the cell itself (if you press [F2])

D7		✕ ✓ ?	29						
	A	B	C	D	E	F	G	H	I
1	Lottery Number Tally Sheet								
2									
3	Date	1st	2nd	3rd	4th	5th	6th	Bonus	Win
4	Sat 2 September 00	3	6	12	29	36	46		£0.00
5		2	9	12	25	26	49		£10.00
6		15	16	33	35	41	45		£0.00
7	Numbers Drawn	3	9	29	30	42	49	22	
8	Total Won								£10.00
9	Date	1st	2nd	3rd	4th	5th	6th	Bonus	Win
10	Sat 9 September 00	3	6	12	29	36	46		£0.00
11		2	9	12	25	26	49		£0.00
12		15	16	33	35	41	45		£0.00
13	Numbers Drawn	4	12	22	32	33	45	10	
14	Total Won								£0.00

Formatting options

Column width/row height

All the columns and rows in a worksheet are a standard width and height unless you adjust them. You should adjust the widths and heights as necessary to get your text and data to fit.

To adjust the width of a column:

- Click and drag the vertical line (in the column heading row) to the right of the column whose width you want to change, e.g. to change the width of column C drag the vertical line between column C and D.

To adjust the column width to give a 'best fit':

- In Excel, double-click the vertical line (in the column-headings) to the right of the column you want to adjust.

A	B	C	D
Room Inventory - September 2000			⬌ ADJUST
Office	**Value**	**Bedroom1**	**Value**
Pine Computer desk	£500	Pine double door unit	£350
Swivelling office chair	£75	Pine 3 drawer bedside cabinets * 2	£500
Pentium PC, 17" monitor, Win 98, Office 2000	£3,000	Kingsize divan with storage, Pine kingsize headboard	£550
Deskjet 870Cxi colour printer	£200	Kingsize electric blanket	£40
Bookcase - pine - 6 shelves	£300	Bed sheets, duvet, pillows etc	£250
Filing cabinet	£200	Bedside lights, shades, uplighter	£150
		Antique pine chest of (4) drawers	£400
	£4,275		**£2,240**

Drag

- In Works, double-click in the column heading row of the column you want to adjust.

You can also adjust the column width or row height from the Format menu.

① Click inside the row or column you want to adjust.

② Open the **Format** menu.

③ In Excel choose **Row** then **Height**, or **Column** then **Width**.

Or

- In Works, choose **Row Height...** or **Column Width...**

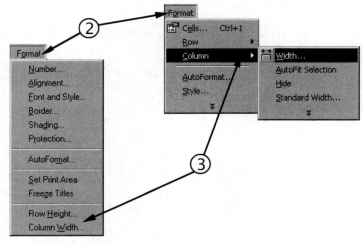

④ Complete the dialog box.

⑤ Click **OK**.

Select the column in Works if you intend to do a **Best Fit** from the **Column Width** dialog box

Alignment and text wrap

Use the alignment tools on the toolbar for horizontal alignment

When entering text into cells you might want to try some other formatting options to help you display your work effectively. These options can be used on any cells, but may be particularly effective on column headings. Options include:

- Horizontal alignment
- Vertical alignment
- Wrap text
- Merge and centre

These options can all be found in the **Format**, **Alignment** dialog box in Works and the **Format Cells** dialog box, on the **Alignment** tab, in Excel.

Try it: Set the alignment and text wrap

① Select the cells you want to format.

② Open the **Format** menu and choose **Alignment** (in Works).

Or

- Choose **Cells...** and select the **Alignment** tab (in Excel).

③ Specify the option(s) required.

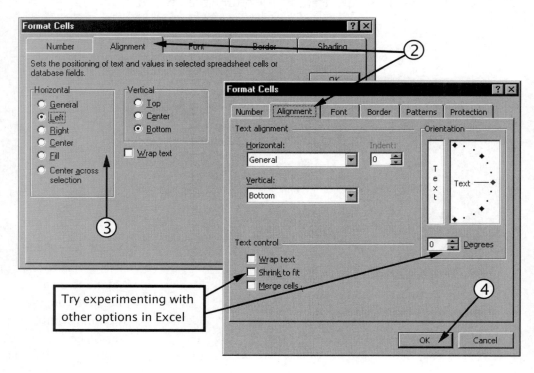

Try experimenting with other options in Excel

④ Click **OK**.

• You may need to adjust the row height or column width if it doesn't adjust automatically to accommodate the alignment options you choose.

Insert/delete rows and columns

If you need to insert a row or column into your worksheet you can easily do so. You can also delete rows and columns.

Try it: Insert and delete rows and columns

To insert a row:

① Select the row that will go *below* the row you are inserting.

② Right-click within the selected area.

③ Choose **Insert** (Excel) or **Insert Row** (Works) from the pop-up menu.

To insert a column:

① Select the column that will go to the right of the column you are inserting.

② Right-click within the selected area.

③ Choose **Insert** (Excel) or **Insert Columns** (Works) from the pop-up menu.

To delete a row or column:

① Select the row or column you wish to delete.

② Right-click within the selected area.

③ Choose **Delete** (Excel) or **Delete Column/Delete Row** in Works.

You can add or delete several rows or columns at the same time if necessary.

① Click and drag in the row or column label area to indicate the number of rows or columns you want to insert or delete.

② Right-click within the selected area.

③ Choose the **Insert** or **Delete** option as required.

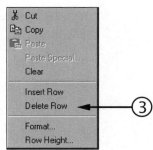

Number formats

A lot of the data entered into a worksheet is currency. If you want the £ symbol in front of a figure you can either:

*   Format the cells to display the data in a currency format.

Or

*   Enter the '£' symbol through the keyboard.

	A	B	C
1	Data entered	Format applied	Result
2	10000	Currency	£ 10,000.00
3	12500	Comma	12,500.00
4	0.15	Percent	15%
5			

If you enter your figures through the numeric keypad, it's probably easiest to format the cells to display the figures as currency.

You can format cells *before* or *after* you have entered your text or data.

Try it: Format cells to display in the currency format

①   Select the cells you want to format.

②   Click the **Currency** tool ☞ on the **Formatting** toolbar.

In Excel, the Formatting toolbar has other tools to help you format your numbers – Percent Style, Comma Style, Increase and Decrease Decimal. Other number formats can be found in the **Format Cells** dialog box, on the **Number** tab – have a look to see if any would be useful to you.

In Works, you will find other number format options in the **Format, Number**... dialog box.

Try it: Apply other number formats using the Format Cells (Excel) or Format Number dialog box (Works):

①   Select the cells to format.

②   Open the **Format** menu.

③   Choose **Cells**... then select the **Number** tab (Excel).

Or

③   Select **Number**... (Works).

④   Choose a category or format from the list, e.g. Currency.

⑤   Complete the dialog box as required.

⑥   Click **OK**.

Formulas

Any cell in your worksheet which will contain a figure that has been calculated using other entries in your workbook, should have a formula in it (do *not* do your calculations on a calculator, then type the answer into your worksheet!!).

Formulas allow you to add, subtract, multiply, divide and work out percentages of the values in cells.

Operators used in formulas are:

+ Add	– Subtract	/ Divide	* Multiply	% Percentage (Excel only)

Formula examples

When you build up formulas, you use addresses to identify the cells that contain the figures you want to work with, e.g.

=B4-C4	Subtract the figure in C4 from the figure in B4
=C3*E4	Multiply the figure in C3 by the figure in E4
=(40/100)*B4	Calculate 40% of the figure in B4
=B4*40%	Find 40% of the value in B4 (Excel only)

You can only normally see the results of formulas, but they can be displayed if required (see page 146)

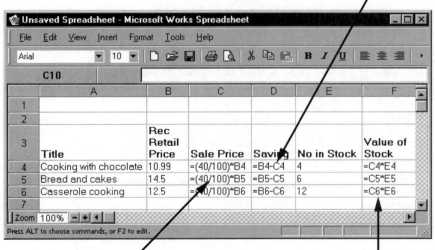

Sale Price is 40% (40/100) of the Retail Price

Value of stock is Sale Price multiplied by No in Stock

Key points on formula construction

Order of precedence

Where a formula contains a mixture of operators, multiplications and divisions will be performed *before* additions and subtractions, e.g. in =A4+C7*D7 the figure in C7 would be multiplied by the one in D7, and then the result would be added to the figure in A4.

Parentheses

You can also make long formulas easier to read by using parentheses

Some formulas can become quite long and complicated.

If you want to force the order in which a formula is worked out (as you would when calculating a percentage in Works), or even just make a long formula easier to read, you must use parentheses ( ).

In the example below, the problem within each set of parentheses is solved *before* working through the formula – you work from the inside to the outside.

=((A1+B2)*C3)) - (D4/E5)

Add A1 to B2	we'll call this *result 1*
Multiply *result 1* by C3	we'll call this *result 2*
Divide D4 by E5	we'll call this *result 3*
Subtract *result 3* from *result 2*	

Entering formulas is easy!

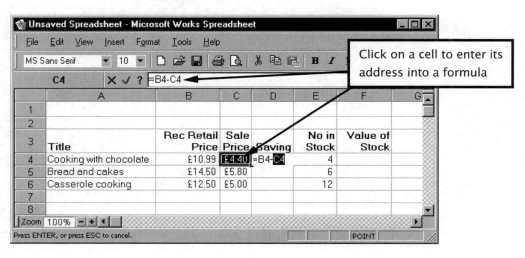

Try it: Entering formulas

① Select the cell that you want to put a formula in.

② Press the = key.

③ Click on the cell that you want in your formula e.g. B4.

④ Press the operator, e.g. –.

⑤ Repeat steps 3 and 4 until you've completed the formula.

⑥ Press **[Enter]**.

Key points to note about entering formulas

• You could type the cell addresses through the keyboard if you prefer, but if you can see the cells that are to be part of the formula it's usually easier to click on them.

• If the formula needs parentheses, type them as you go.

AutoFill

AutoFill can be used to copy formulas down columns or across rows. In this screenshot, the formula in cell D4 is =B4-C4. We need a similar formula in the other cells in the column. You can complete the cells using a feature called AutoFill.

Try it: Use AutoFill

① Select **D4**.

② Position the pointer over the bottom right corner of the cell – the **Fill Handle** (a small black cross) should appear.

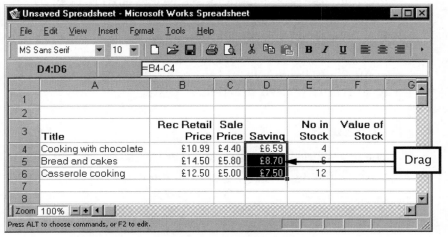

③ Click and drag the black cross down over the other *Saving* cells.

When you release the mouse, the formula in cell D4 will be copied to the cells you dragged over.

If you click on each cell in the *Saving* column and keep an eye on the Formula bar, you will notice that the formula has automatically changed *relative* to the position you have copied the formula to.

You can also use AutoFill to automatically generate days of the week and months of the year.

Try it: Use AutoFill with months and days

① Enter January, Monday or Mon in any cell.

② AutoFill it down or across.

	A	B	C	D
8				
9	January	Mon	**Monday**	
10	February	Tue	**Tuesday**	
11	March	Wed	**Wednesday**	
12	April	Thu	**Thursday**	
13	May	Fri	**Friday**	
14				
15				

Functions

Both Works and Excel have a considerable range of functions for your use. The functions make it relatively easy to perform long or complex calculations on your data. Explore the functions in your application to see if there are any that you would find useful.

AutoSum (which inserts the Sum function) is perhaps the most regularly used function.

AutoSum

The next worksheet contains details of share purchases made.

To calculate the total amount spent on shares we could use a formula e.g. =G4+G5+G6+G7+G8, but the easiest and quickest way to calculate the total is to use *AutoSum*.

Try it: Calculate totals using AutoSum (adjacent cells)

① Select a cell in which you want a total to appear, e.g. the cell that will contain the total amount spent on shares.

② Click the **AutoSum** tool Σ on the **Standard** toolbar.

③ The range of cells that are going to be added together will be highlighted. Note that the function also appears in the Formula bar.

④ If the suggested range of cells is correct, press [Enter].

G4:G9	✗ ✓ ?	=SUM(G4:G9)					
	A	B	C	D	E	F	G
1	**Share Purchases**						
2							
3	Purchase Date	Company	No of shares	Ask Price	Comm ission	Stamp Duty	Total Purchase Cost
4	08/04/00	Lloyds TSB	750	£5.74	£15.00	£14.34	£4,330.59
5	22/06/00	Rolls Royce	1500	£1.70	£15.00	£8.49	£2,569.74
6	03/06/00	Thus	1000	£0.66	£15.00	£3.30	£678.30
7	03/04/00	Dixons	1000	£3.53	£17.65	£17.65	£3,565.30
8	25/08/00	Stagecoach	1000	£2.28	£15.00	£11.38	£2,301.38
9							
10							=SUM(G4:G9)
11							

- If the suggested range is *not* the range you want to add together, drag over the correct range, then press [Enter].

- The total value of the selected range of cells will appear in the active cell when you hit [Enter].

You can also use AutoSum to total non-adjacent cells.

Try it: Total non-adjacent cells

① Select the cell that will contain the result of the calculation.

② Click the **AutoSum** tool on the **Standard** toolbar.

③ Click on the first cell that you want to include in the range of cells.

④ Enter a , (comma).

⑤ Repeat steps 3 and 4 until you've specified all the cells required (don't put a comma after the last cell address).

⑥ Press [Enter].

Formula palette – Excel only

The Formula Palette is used to help you enter your formulas and functions. Have a look at the Formula Palette – it makes the generation of formulas relatively easy!

- To display the Formula Palette, click the **Edit Formula** button (the = sign) to the left of the Formula bar.

- To change the function being used, click the drop-down arrow to display the function list, and select a different function.

- If the Formula Palette obscures the area of the worksheet you want to view, click the button to the right of a data entry field – the Formula Palette will become minimised, so you can see your worksheet.

- To display the palette again, click the **Restore Formula Palette** button at the right side of the minimised window.

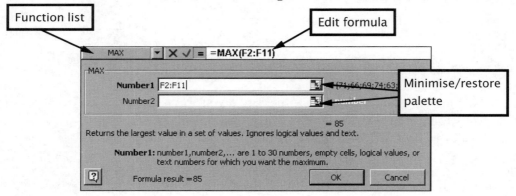

Statistical functions

Statistical functions include minimum, maximum, average, count – and many others.

These can be used to display a value from a range of cells.

- To return the minimum value from a range use: **MIN**
- To return the maximum value from a range use: **MAX**
- To return the average value from a range use: **AVERAGE**
- To count the number of entries in a range use: **COUNT**

Try it: Use statistical functions (Excel)

① Select the cell that the function will go in.

② Open the **Formula Palette** (click the **Edit Formula** button).

③ Select the function from the list, and jump to step 7.

④ If the function is not on the list, click **More Functions**... to display the **Paste Function** dialog box.

⑤ Select a category from the **Function category** list.

• If a function has been used recently, it will be in the most recently used list. If you're not sure what category a function is in, select the *All* category (every function is listed here, in alphabetical order). Minimum, Maximum, Average and Count can be found in the *Statistical* category.

⑥ Scroll through the **Function name** list, select the function you require and click **OK**.

⑦ Enter the range of cells you want the function to operate on – either drag over the range, or type the cell addresses (minimise the Palette to see the sheet if necessary).

⑧ Restore the Formula Palette if necessary.

⑨ Click **OK**.

Try it: statistical functions (Works)

① Select the cell that the function will go in.

② Open the **Insert** menu and choose **Function**.

③ Select the function category.

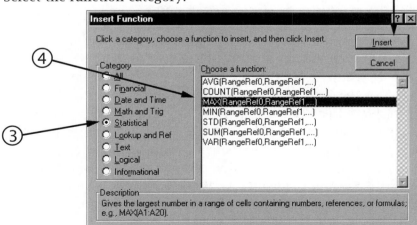

④　Choose the function.

⑤　Click **Insert**.

⑥　Select the prompt (RangeRef0, RangeRef1) within the parentheses.

⑦　**Drag over the cells** you want the function to work on.

⑧　Press [Enter].

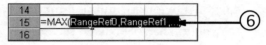

14	
15	=MAX(RangeRef0,RangeRef1 ,...)
16	

View formula

If you wish to view the formulas and functions that are in your worksheet, rather than the results of the calculations, you can toggle the display at any time.

Excel:

•　Press **[Ctrl] –[|]**

Works:

•　Open the **View menu** and choose **Formulas**.

14		
15	Minimum	=MIN(F4:F13)
16	Maximum	=MAX(F4:F13)
17	Average	=AVERAGE(F4:F13)
18	Count	=COUNT(F4:F13)
19		
20		

Relative and absolute addresses

Relative addresses change automatically when you copy a formula. Absolute address remain constant.

When you AutoFill or copy a formula or function, the cell addresses used in the formula or function change automatically, relative to the position you copy them to. By default, the cell addresses used are *relative addresses*.

There may be times when you use a cell address in a formula or function, but you don't want the cell address to change relative to its new position if it is AutoFilled or copied. To stop the cell address changing when it is copied, it must be made into an *absolute address*. An absolute address will not change when the formula or function containing it is copied or moved.

To create an absolute cell address:

- Enter a $ sign in front of each co-ordinate you do not want to change.

You can enter the $ sign by typing it in through the keyboard.

Try it: Use an absolute address for a cell in a formula

① Select the cell that contains the formula.

② Click in the Formula bar.

③ Type a $ sign in front of each coordinate that you want to make absolute.

④ Press [Enter].

	A	B	C	D	E	F
11	Value of shares - assuming growth of 5%				1.05	
12		To buy	Now worth			
13	Lloyds TSB	£4,301.25	£4,516.31			
14	Rolls Royce	£2,546.25	£2,673.56			
15	Thus	£660.00	£693.00			
16	Dixons	£3,530.00	£3,706.50			
17	Stagecoach	£2,275.00	£2,388.75			

	A	B	C
11	Value of shares - assu		
12		To buy	Now worth
13	Lloyds TSB	=C4*D4	=B13*E11
14	Rolls Royce	=C5*D5	=B14*E11
15	Thus	=C6*D6	=B15*E11
16	Dixons	=C7*D7	=B16*E11
17	Stagecoach	=C8*D8	=B17*E11

If you AutoFill or copy the formula, you should find that the absolutely addressed part of the formula or function doesn't change.

B2	neither co-ordinate will change if copied or moved
B$2	the column will change
$B2	the row number will change
B2	both co-ordinates will change relative to the new position

Sort

If you've typed a list of data into your spreadsheet you may want to sort it into ascending or descending order on a specific column. You can perform alphabetic or numeric sorts on your data. A simple sort will sort the data on one column only, and in a multilevel sort you can sort on up to three columns at a time.

Try it: Perform a simple sort in Excel

① Select any cell in the column you want to base your sort on.

② Click the **Sort Ascending** 📊 or **Sort Descending** 📊 tool on the **Standard** toolbar.

Try it: a simple sort in Works

① Select the data you want to sort.

② Open the **Tools menu** and choose **Sort**...

③ Select the option from the **Sort** dialog box and click **OK**.

④ Specify the column you want to sort by.

⑤ Select the sort order – ascending or descending.

⑥ Do you want the first row in the selected data to be sorted? If not (if it contains your column headings), select the **My list has Header row** option.

⑦ Click **Sort**.

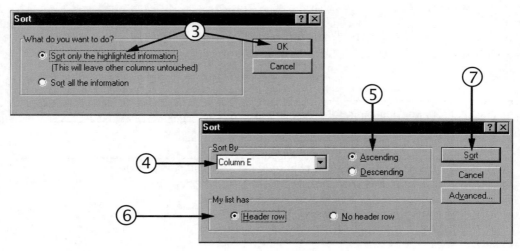

To sort on more than one field, use a multilevel sort.

Try it: Multilevel sort

① Select the range of cells that you want to sort.

② Open the **Tools menu** and choose **Sort**...

Works only

③ Select the option required from the **Sort** dialog box and click **OK**.

④ Click **Advanced**... in the **Sort** dialog box.

Works and Excel

⑤ Set up the sort criteria.

⑥ Click **Sort** (Works) or **OK** (Excel).

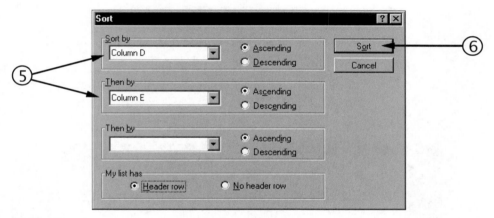

Charts

Bar graphs, line graphs, pie charts, scatter diagrams, etc. can be produced from the data in your worksheet. The chart is placed on a chart sheet in your file (although in Excel you can create your chart as an object on the same worksheet as the data on which the chart is built if you wish).

Producing a chart is quite easy, and the results can be very effective

Key points to note when charting

• Data that you want to chart should be in cells that are next to each other.

• If the data you want to chart has blank rows or columns within it, remove these before you try to chart the data.

Works

① Select the data that you want to chart – including column headings and row labels (the text in these will be used for your legend and the x-axis labels).

Explore the Edit and Format menus when viewing your chart in Works – there are several chart formatting options in them

A3:D8					
	A	B	C	D	E	F
1	SALES FIGURES (1st Quarter 1999)					
2						
3		JAN	FEB	MAR	TOTAL	
4	Gill Burns	£10,124	£12,452	£14,090	£36,666	
5	Peter Collins	£12,400	£13,769	£15,089	£41,258	
6	Paula Duncan	£9,670	£17,324	£12,400	£39,394	
7	Jim Ferguson	£10,134	£12,908	£16,500	£39,542	
8	Ann Mitchell	£11,340	£12,050	£14,000	£37,390	
9	TOTAL	£53,668	£68,503	£72,079	£194,250	
10						

② Click the **New Chart** tool ▮.

③ If the **First Time Help** dialog box appears, click **OK**.

④ Select the **Basic Options** tab if necessary.

⑤ Choose a chart type, enter a heading, switch the chart border and gridlines on or off as required, etc.

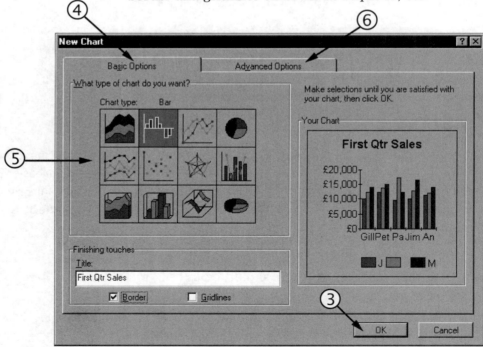

⑥ Select the **Advanced Options** tab and experiment with the options to see if you can improve your chart.

⑦ Click **OK** when you've finished.

• Your chart will be displayed in its own window.

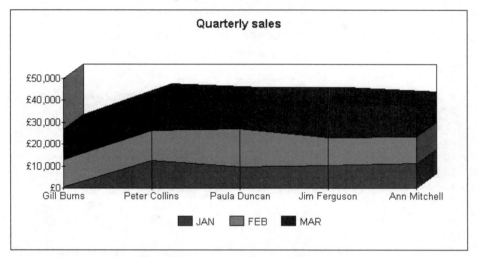

When you are at your chart you can use the tools on the toolbar to return to the Chart Type dialog box so that you can change your settings.

To move from your chart to your spreadsheet:

• Open the **View** menu and choose **Spreadsheet**.

To move from your spreadsheet to your chart:

• Open the **View** menu and choose **Chart** (if you have created more than one chart from your data, a dialog box will be displayed so you can choose which chart you want to display).

Key points to note

• If you make any changes to the data in the spreadsheet, the chart will be updated automatically.

Excel

In Excel, you can use the Chart Wizard to step you through the process of setting up your chart.

The quickest way to produce a chart using the default chart layout is to select the data for charting then press [F11]

Try it: Use the Chart Wizard

① Select the data you want to chart – including the column headings and row labels.

② Click the **Chart Wizard** tool on the **Standard** toolbar.

③ At step 1 of the Chart Wizard, select the **Chart type**.

• Click the **Press and Hold to View Sample** button to see what your data would look like in your chosen chart type.

④ Once you've decided on a type, click **Next**.

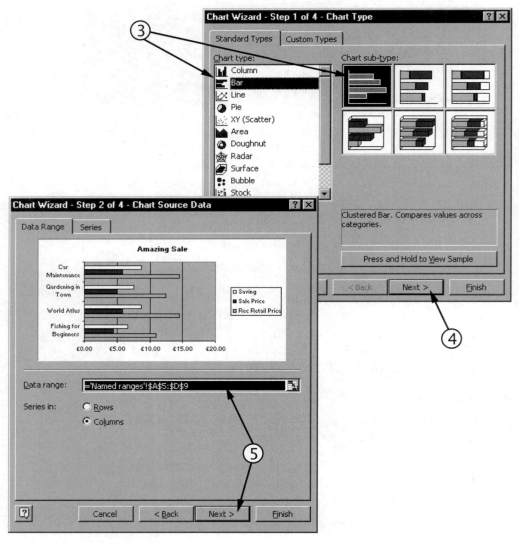

⑤ At step 2, on the **Data Range** tab, check the data range selected, decide whether you want to display the data series in rows or columns (try both and decide which you prefer). Click **Next**.

⑥ At step 3, explore the tabs in the **Chart Options** dialog box and set your options. Click **Next** to move on.

⑦ Finally, decide where the chart should be located (the chart looks best on a new Chart sheet) and click **Finish**.

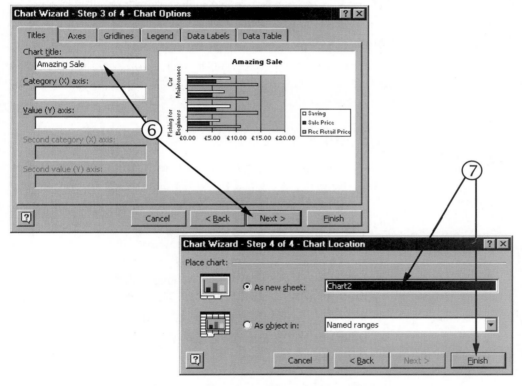

• When you are working with a chart, the Chart toolbar is displayed and a Chart menu appears on the menu bar.

Chart toolbar

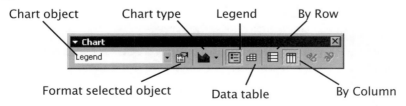

From the chart menu:

Chart Type...	Displays the dialog box from Step 1 of the Wizard. You get access to all the chart types and sub-types from here.
Source Data...	Displays the dialog box from Step 2. Use this to edit the data range.
Chart Options...	Displays the dialog box from Step 3. You can add titles, change the position of the legend, edit the gridlines, etc. through this box.
Location...	Displays the dialog box from Step 4. Change the location of the chart from here – move it to a new sheet, or put it on a Chart sheet.

Chart objects

Each area of your chart is an object – you have a chart area object, plot area object, category axis object, value axis object, legend object, etc.

Formatting chart objects

You can change the formatting of each object in your chart to get the effect you want – you might want to change the colours of the bars in a bar chart, or change the position of the legend.

- To format an object in your chart, double-click on it. When the **Format** dialog box appears, explore it to see the various formatting options you have. Experiment with the options until you find the right formatting for your chart.

- If you want to format the font of an object, you can use the tools on the **Formatting** toolbar – font, font size, bold, italic, etc.

To change the chart type

If your chart doesn't look the way you expected, and you think a different chart type would be better, you can change the chart type at any time.

To change the chart type:

① Click the drop down arrow to the right of the Chart Type tool on the **Chart** toolbar.

② Select the type of chart required.

A chart in your worksheet

If you opt to insert your chart as an object in a worksheet, the **Chart** toolbar should be displayed when you return to the worksheet.

• The chart will be selected – there will be *handles* in each corner and along each side.

• If you click on the worksheet area, the chart becomes de-selected, and the **Chart** toolbar disappears.

• To select the chart again, click on it once.

Move, resize and delete chart

If you want to move, resize or delete a chart you must first select the *Chart Area* – either point to the chart area within the chart and click (a prompt will tell you what the mouse is pointing at) or choose Chart Area from the chart object list on the **Chart** toolbar.

To move the chart:

① Select the chart.

② Point to the Chart Area using the mouse – a prompt will appear to tell you what area of the chart you are point-ing at.

③ Drag the chart to its new position.

To resize the chart:

① Select the chart. Point to one of the handles along the edge of the chart area.

② Drag the handle to increase or decrease the size of the object.

To delete the chart:

① Select the chart.

② Press [Delete].

Preview, Page layout and print

At some stage you will want to print your file. Before sending a worksheet to print, it's a good idea to *preview* it. Previewing the file gives you the opportunity to check that your worksheet will fit well on the page – if it doesn't you can do something about it before you print.

Print Preview

You cannot edit a worksheet in Print Preview. You must close the preview window and return to your worksheet if you wish to change something.

Try it: Take your worksheet into Print Preview

• Click the Print Preview tool .

Page Setup options

You might need to change some of the Page Setup options for your worksheet to get your printout just as you want it. You can access the options by choose **Page Setup**... from the **File** menu. If you are using Excel, you can also display the **Page Setup** dialog box from the Print Preview window by clicking the **Setup**... button on the **Print Preview** toolbar.

Orientation

You can print a page either portrait (tall) or landscape (wide):

① Select the **Page tab** (Excel) or the **Source, Size & Orientation tab** (Works).

② Choose the orientation option required.

③ Click **OK**.

Scaling (Excel only)

If your worksheet has the last few rows or columns on a new page and you'd rather they fitted onto the previous page with the rest of your data, you can specify the number of pages to print on to using the **Scaling** options.

① Select the **Page** tab.

② In the **Scaling** options, specify the number of pages wide and tall you want your worksheet to fit on.

③ Click **OK**.

Page size

The default paper size is A4. You can select an alternative.

① Select the **Page** tab (Excel) or the **Source, Size & Orientation** tab (Works).

② Choose the paper size required for the **Paper size** list.

③ Click **OK**.

Margins

The margins are the white space between the edge of your paper and your data. To increase or decrease the margins:

① Select the **Margins** tab.

② Specify the margins you want to use.

③ Click **OK**.

Headers and footers (Excel only)

Headers and footers display information at the top or bottom of every page that prints out for your worksheet. You can format headers and footers from the **Custom Header** or **Custom Footer** dialog box.

① Select the **Header/Footer** tab.

② Choose a header or footer from the lists and click **OK**.

Or

• Click **Custom Header…** or **Custom Footer…**

If you choose Custom Header… or Custom Footer…:

① Click in the section you want your header or footer to appear in – left, centre or right.

② Type your text or click a button to add page numbers, date, time, etc.

③ Select the text or field entered and format it as required (click the **Font** button – the first one in the dialog box).

④ Click **OK**.

Headers and footers (Works only)

① Open the View menu and choose **Headers and Footers**.

② Complete the **View Headers and Footers** dialog box as required and click **OK**.

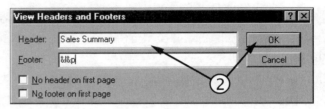

Print

When you are happy with the preview of your worksheet, you can send it to print.

• From your worksheet or from Print Preview in Works, click the **Print** tool to print one copy of the worksheet.

If you are in Print Preview in Excel:

① Click **Print**... on the Print Preview toolbar.

② Complete the **Print** dialog box – specify the **Print range, Copies** and **Print what** options as required.

③ Click **OK**.

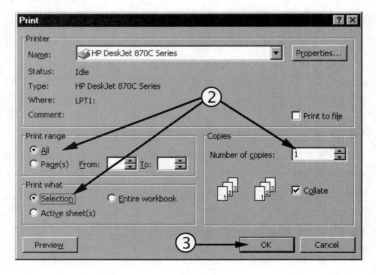

Print part of your worksheet

If you don't want to print all of your worksheet, you can print the area required on its own.

Try it: Print part of your worksheet (Excel)

① Select the range of cells you want to print.

② Open the **File menu** and choose **Print**...

③ Select **Selection** from the **Print what** options.

④ Click **OK**.

Try it: Print part of your worksheet (Works)

① Select the range of cells you want to print.

② Choose **Set Print Area** from the **Format** menu.

③ Click **OK**.

④ Preview and print as normal.

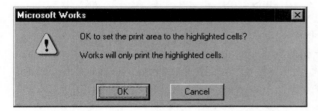

To cancel the print area, select the whole worksheet (click the box where the row numbers and column headings meet), open the **Format** menu and choose **Set Print Area**.

Printing your chart

You can print your chart with or without the data on which is based.

To print a chart that is an object within your worksheet you have several options. I suggest you do a Print Preview before you actually print, just to check it looks okay.

To print out all of the data on the worksheet *and* the chart, print the worksheet as normal (with the chart deselected).

To get a printout of the chart only:

• Select the chart on the worksheet, then print.

To get the chart, plus the data on which it is based, but no other data from the worksheet:

① Select the chart.

② Click the **Data Table** tool ⊞ on the **Chart** toolbar to display the data table for the chart.

③ Print out with the chart selected.

To print a chart that is on a separate Chart sheet:

① Select the Chart sheet.

② Print as usual.

• If you also want to print out the data on which the chart is based, display the Data Table before you print.

• In Excel, you can use the drawing tools to create different effects on your worksheet data and charts. If you create charts, try using an Arrow and a Text Box to add emphasis to it!

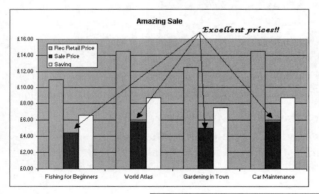

Column chart, with arrows and text box (created in Excel)

Pie chart, with data labels (created in Works)

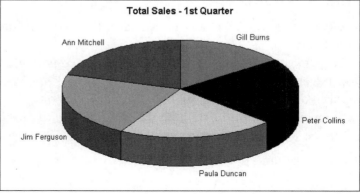

7
Databases

IN THIS CHAPTER:

- Database jargon
- Table structure
- Entering and editing data
- Forms
- Find, sort and filter
- Printouts and reports

If you have data that you want to be able to find, organise and print then you need a database package. You could catalogue your CDs or books, keep track of customer information or set up a membership database for your club. This chapter discusses databases, with examples from Works and Access. The Works database is a very neat yet simple database that can sort, filter and produce reports easily. Access is aimed at the business market – it's full of sophisticated features bursting to get out!

Database jargon

Databases use their own jargon! Some of the terminology may be unfamiliar to you so I've listed brief definitions of the terms you are likely to encounter in the near future.

Term	Definition
Table	The data in your database is stored in a table. In a simple database, you might have only one table. More complex databases may consist of several tables. A Works database consists of one table only – an Access database may contain several tables.
Record	A record contains information about a single item in your table. All the information relating to a book, CD or member of staff will be held in a separate record.
Field	A field is a piece of data within a record. If you are storing data about the books in your library, you would set up separate fields for ISBN, title, author, publisher, etc.

It doesn't matter what database package you use, the jargon is very similar

- Each RECORD in a table is presented in a ROW;
- Each FIELD in a record is in a COLUMN;
- Each field has a FIELD NAME at the top of the column.

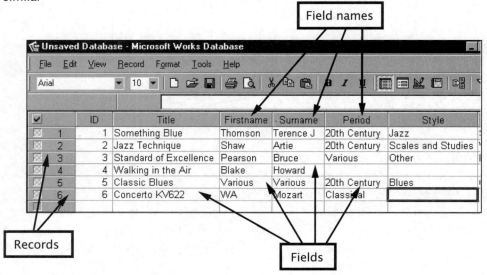

Field names

Records

Fields

Objects

A database consists of *objects* that can be used to input, display, interrogate, print and automate your work. In Access, the objects are listed in the Database Window. In Works you can change views to display the various objects. The objects that will be mentioned in this chapter are summarised below:

Tables	Tables are the most important objects in your Database. Tables are used for data entry and editing.
Queries	You use Queries to sort, extract groups of records that meet specific criteria and to perform calculations.
Forms	Forms provide an alternative view of the data in your tables. You can enter and edit data using a form, though the data is still stored in a Table.
Reports	Reports allow you to arrange your data attractively ready for printing. You can print your data out directly from your Table, but a report looks more professional and is often easier to read – it's more 'user friendly'!

There are also macros and modules in Access, but we won't discuss them in this book.

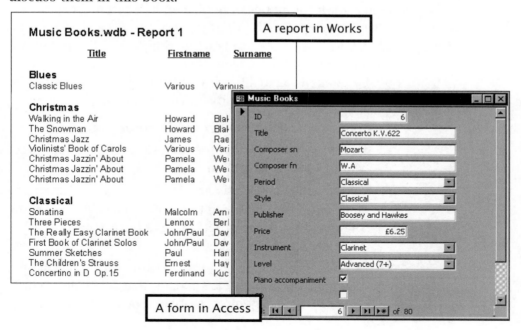

A report in Works

Music Books.wdb - Report 1

	Title	Firstname	Surname
Blues			
	Classic Blues	Various	Various
Christmas			
	Walking in the Air	Howard	Blak
	The Snowman	Howard	Blak
	Christmas Jazz	James	Rae
	Violinists' Book of Carols	Various	Vari
	Christmas Jazzin' About	Pamela	We
	Christmas Jazzin' About	Pamela	We
	Christmas Jazzin' About	Pamela	We
Classical			
	Sonatina	Malcolm	Arn
	Three Pieces	Lennox	Berl
	The Really Easy Clarinet Book	John/Paul	Dav
	First Book of Clarinet Solos	John/Paul	Dav
	Summer Sketches	Paul	Har
	The Children's Strauss	Ernest	Hay
	Concertino in D Op.15	Ferdinand	Kuc

Music Books

ID	6
Title	Concerto K.V.622
Composer sn	Mozart
Composer fn	W.A
Period	Classical
Style	Classical
Publisher	Boosey and Hawkes
Price	£6.25
Instrument	Clarinet
Level	Advanced (7+)
Piano accompaniment	☑
	☐

6 of 80

A form in Access

Table structure

Planning and design

Planning your database is very important – take your time and think it through

A simple database could be used to record name and address details (e.g. your Christmas card list). You could also use a database to store and manage details of your CD or book collection, or to organise the data you need to run your company (suppliers, customers, stock, order details etc).

In a simple database, it may be feasible to store all the information together in one table – perhaps with a Christmas card list or a list of music books (the example used in this chapter). Other databases will be more complex and may require several tables. A Works database has one table only.

Preparing your data

Before you set up a database you should decide what you want to be able to do with it. If you intend to record details of the books held in your library, you might want to be able to produce lists of all books by a particular author, or on a particular topic, or all books published in a certain year.

Once you've decided what you want to do with your database, you will be able to start working out what fields you need in your table or tables. If you are setting up a database of the books in your library you would perhaps want book title, author, publisher, subject, year published, price, etc.

Key points to consider when deciding on your fields

- Create a separate field for each item of data you might want to sort or search on.

- Break names up into separate fields, e.g. Title, First name and Last name. If you do this, you will be able to sort the file into Last name order, or search for someone using the First name and Last name.

- Addresses – use separate fields for Street, Town/City, Region and/or Country. You can then sort your records into order on any of these fields, or locate records by specifying appropriate search criteria. For example, using Street and Town/City fields, you could search for details of people who live in St John's Street (Street), Stirling (Town/City) rather than St John's Street, Dundee.

When planning your database, take a small sample of the data you wish to store and examine it carefully. This will help you to confirm what fields will be required.

Creating a database in Access

When you start Access, the copyright screen will appear for a few seconds, followed by the Microsoft Access dialog box.

Creating a database in Works is discussed on page 170

① Choose **Blank Access database** at the Microsoft Access dialog box and click **OK**.

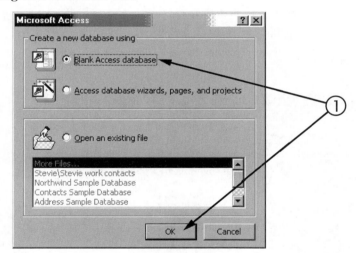

You will arrive at the **File New Database** dialog box.

② Decide where you want to store your database (*My Documents* is the default).

As with all Microsoft packages, a temporary filename is suggested for your database – in Access this follows the pattern *db1*, *db2*, *db3* in each working session. You need to replace the temporary name with a name that means something to you, and reflects the contents of your database.

③ Give your database a name and click the **Create** button.

Your database is created and the database window is displayed – you are ready to start setting up your database.

The Access screen

You should be able to identify the following areas within the Access application window:

- Application Title bar
- Menu bar
- Status bar
- Database toolbar
- Database window
- Application Minimise, Maximise/Restore and Close buttons

Within the Database window you can see:

- Database Title bar
- Groups bar (Access 2000)
- Database window toolbar
- Objects bar
- New object shortcuts
- Database Minimise, Maximise/Restore and Close buttons

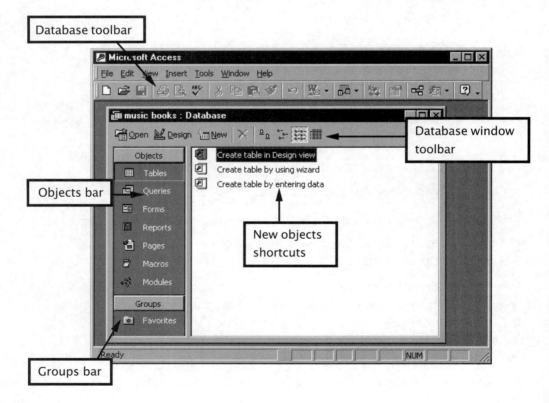

Creating a new table

① **Select Tables** in the Objects Bar.

② Double-click **Create table in Design view**.

In Design view you can specify the field names, data types and any other properties you think would be useful.

To enter the table design:

③ Type the field name into the **Field Name** column.

④ Select a Data Type from the options available in the **Data Type** column.

⑤ The **Description** column is optional – anything typed here will be displayed on the Status bar at the data entry stage.

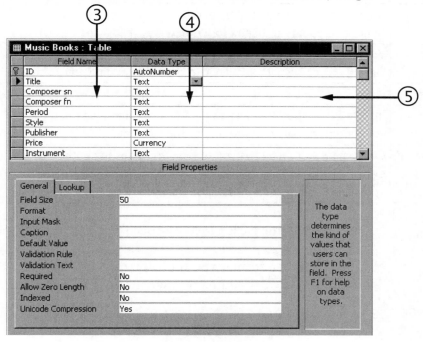

Key points to note

* In Access you must create a Database file before you can set up your tables;

* An Access database may consist of many tables;

* In Works, a database consists of one table only.

Field data types and properties

There are 10 different data types to choose from when setting up your table structures in Access. Brief notes on each type are given in the table below. Most of your fields will probably be Text, with a few of the others used in each table depending on the type of data you wish to store.

Data Type usage

Text	Alphanumeric data. Default data type.
Memo	Alphanumeric data – sentences and paragraphs. Cannot be indexed.
Number	Numeric data
Date/Time	Dates and times. Values for the years 100 through to 9999.
Currency	Monetary data.
Auto Number	Unique number generated by Access for each new record. Cannot be updated. Useful for Primary Key fields (see below)
Yes/No	Yes and No values, and fields that contain one of 2 values – On/Off, True/False. Displayed as a checkbox at data entry stage.
OLE Object	Pictures, graphs or other objects from another Windows application.
Hyperlink	Inserts a 'hot spot' that lets you jump to another location on your computer, on your intranet or the Internet.
Lookup Wizard	Creates a field that allows you to look up values in another table or from a combo box (drop-down list). Choosing this option starts the Lookup Wizard to define the data type.

Try setting up a basic table structure for your books or CDs, or copy the example given for music books on page 170

You can customise each field by specifying different properties in the lower pane of the **Table Design** window, e.g. the field size or the format you want the data displayed in. The properties vary depending on the data type you choose.

Primary Key

Most of the tables that you set up in Access will have a field within them that is unique in each record. It may be an ISBN number field in a book table, or the registration number of a car if you are recording details of company cars. This field should be designated the Primary Key for the table. The information held in a Primary Key field will be different in each record. Give the field that will become a Primary Key an appropriate name, e.g. ISBN, CarReg, StaffID, Student Number, or simply ID.

* To establish Primary Key status, click the **Primary Key** tool 🔑 when the insertion point is anywhere in the Primary Key field row in the upper pane.

The contents of a Primary Key field are different in each record

The Index property is automatically set to *Yes(No Duplicates)* when a field is given Primary Key status. A Primary Key field cannot contain duplicate values within the table.

Save the table design

Once you've specified the table design, you should save it.

① Click the **Save** tool on the **Table design** toolbar.

② Give your table a name, e.g. '*music*'.

③ Click **OK**.

Once the table design has been saved, you can either close the table and return to the database window, or go into Datasheet view so that you can enter your data.

See page 172 for information on data entry

To go into Datasheet view:

* Click the **View** tool ▦ ▾ on the **Table Design** toolbar.

To close the Table Design window and return to the database window:

* Click the **Close** button in the **Table Design** window.

  Your new table will be listed under Tables in the Database window.

Try it: Set up a database table

You could try setting up the following table in your database application. Field types have been suggested for Access and Works – you could use the online Help to get information on any field type you want to find out more about.

Click the New tool to create a new database from within the application

Sheet music/music books database		
Field name	**Data Type – Access**	**Data Type – Works**
ID	AutoNumber (for automatic completion) or Text. Primary Key	Serialized (for automatic completion) or Text
Title	Text	Text
Composer s/n	Text	Text
Composer f/n	Text	Text
Period	Text	Text
Style	Text	Text
Publisher	Text	Text
Price	Currency	Number, Currency format
Instrument	Text	Text
Level	Text	Text
Piano Acc	Yes/No	Number, True/False format
CD	Yes/No	Number, True/False format
Notes	Memo	

Press **[F6]** to switch between the upper and lower pane in Access. Use the lower pane to specify any properties that you consider necessary
Press **[F1]** for help on the data types and properties

Starting Works and setting up your database

① Start the Microsoft Works database – **Start ▶ Programs ▶ Microsoft Works ▶ Microsoft Works Database**

② Select **Blank Database** at the Microsoft Works Database dialog box.

③ Click **OK**.

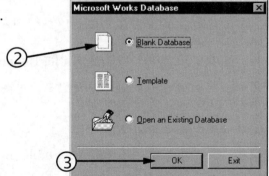

Or, if you are at the Microsoft Works Task Launcher screen:

① Select **Programs** in the **Task Launcher** window.

② Select **Works Database**.

③ Click **Start a blank Database**.

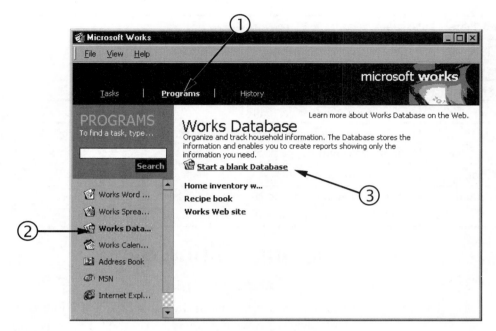

- The **Create Database** dialog box will be displayed.

④ Type in the **name** of your field (up to 15 characters).

⑤ Select a **Format** (and an **Appearance** option if relevant).

⑥ Click **Add**.

⑦ Repeat steps 4-7 until all fields have been added.

⑧ Click **Done**.

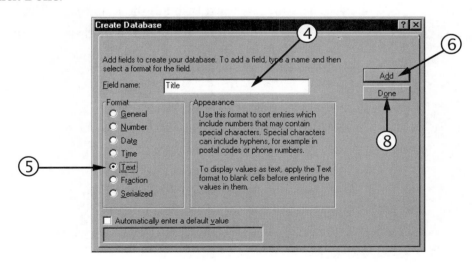

Data Type	Usage
General	Text fields aligned to left, numbers to right
Number	Currency
Date	Several date formats are available
Time	Several time formats available
Text	For fields containing text or text and numbers/special characters, e.g. phone numbers, post codes, addresses
Fraction	Several formats available
Serialized F	For fields that you want to be completed automatically in a set sequence, e.g. 1, 2, 3, or 001, 002, 003

Entering and editing data

Data entry is quite straightforward.

• In Access open your table in Datasheet view. If you are at the Database window, double-click on the table name, or select the table required in the Tables list and click **Open**. The table will be displayed in Datasheet view.

• In Works, an empty table is displayed when you click the **Done** button once you've specified the table structure.

A table looks similar to a spreadsheet layout – each record is presented in a row and each field is in a column.

• To move forward through the fields press the [Tab] key.

• To move backward through the fields press [Shift]-[Tab].

• Or, click in the field you want to move to.

Try it: Enter data

① Type your data into the first field.

② Press the **[Tab]** key to move to the next field.

③ Enter your data.

④ Press **[Tab]**.

⑤ Repeat steps 3 and 4 to complete all the fields.

When you complete the last field in your first record, press [Tab] to move onto the next one.

Editing the table contents

In Access, at the bottom left of the table window, you will find a set of navigation buttons that you can use to move through your table in Datasheet view.

New record tool

- The number field tells you which record you are currently in; the total number of records is on the right.

You can use the scroll bars (horizontal and vertical), to scroll a record into view. Once the record has been located, the simplest technique is to click within the field that needs to be changed and insert or delete data as necessary.

In Works, and in Access if the field contents are selected, press the [F2] key to edit the contents.

Add record

New records can be added to your list of records.

Try it: Add new records
① Scroll through until you display the first empty row under your records (in Access click the New Record ▶✱ tool).
② Enter your record details into the first empty row.

To insert a new record at any position in a Works table:
① Click in the record that will be below the new one.
② Click the **Insert Record** tool 🖹 on the toolbar.
③ Enter the details.

Delete record

Records that are no longer required can be removed.

Try it: Delete a record
Access
① Select the record (click the grey selection bar to its left).

② Press [Delete].

③ Confirm the delete when prompted.

Works

① Click inside the record you want to delete.

② Open the **Record** menu.

③ Click **Delete Record**.

Change the record structure

If you discover a problem with your table design, e.g. you've specified the wrong data type, you can amend the structure.

Try it: Change the record structure (Access)

To move between Datasheet and Design view click the View tool 🖽 ▾

① Click **Tables** in the Objects bar in the Database window.

② Select the table whose design you wish to change.

③ Click 🖋 Design .

④ Edit as necessary and save the changes.

⑤ Close Design view.

To add a new field between two existing fields:

① Place the insertion point in the upper pane anywhere within the field that will go below your new field.

② Click the **Insert Rows** tool ᴴᶜ – a new empty row is inserted above the one the insertion point is in.

③ Enter the field name, data type, etc. as required.

To delete a field

The methods used to add and delete fields in Access and Works are different

① Place the insertion point in the upper pane within the field to be deleted.

② Click the **Delete Rows** tool ᴴ⁺ .

③ Confirm the deletion when prompted.

Try it: Change the record structure (Works)

① Display your list of records if necessary.

② Put the insertion point in the column of the field to be altered.

③ Open the **Format** menu.

④ Choose **Field**...

⑤ Select the **Field** tab.

⑥ Make the changes required.

⑦ Click **OK**.

To add a new field

① Click inside the field you wish to enter a new field next to.

② Open the **Record** menu.

③ Choose **Insert Field**.

④ Choose **Before**... or **After**... (as appropriate).

⑤ Enter the field details.

⑥ Click **Add**.

⑦ Repeat if you want more than one field.

⑧ Click **Done**.

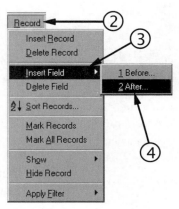

To delete a field

① Click inside the field you want to delete.

② Open the **Record** menu.

③ Choose **Delete Field**.

④ Click **OK**.

• Be careful when you delete fields – when you delete a field you delete it for every record.

Move field

In Access, go into Datasheet view; in Works display your list of records.

① Select the field – click the field name at the top of the column.

② With the pointer in the **Field Name** row, drag the field into its new position – a thick dark vertical line indicates the position that the field will move to.

③ Release the mouse when the line is where you want it.

ID	Title	Firstname	Surname	Period	Style
1	Something Blue	Terence J	Thompson	20th Century	Jazz
2	Jazz Technique	Artie	Shaw	20th Century	Scales and Studies
3	Standard of Excellence	Bruce	Pearson	Various	Other
4	Walking in the Air	Howard	Blake	20th Century	Christmas
5	Classic Blues	Various	Various	20th Century	Blues
6	Concerto K.V.622	W.A	Mozart	Classical	Classical
7	Scales and Arpeggios	Ian	Denley		Scales and Studies
8	100 No.1 Hits	Various	Various	20th Century	Pop
9	Microjazz	Christopher	Norton	20th Century	Jazz
10	Team Woodwind	Cormac/Richard	Loane/Duckett	Various	Other
11	Disney Movie Magic	Various	Various	20th Century	Movie
12	Jazzin' About	Pamela	Wedgwood	20th Century	Jazz

Record: 1 of 80

Formatting options

Experiment with the formatting options available in your application

If you don't like the formatting options on your table you can always try something else.

Try it: Format your table

① Open the Format menu and choose **Font...** (in Access) or **Font and Style** (in Works).

② Complete the dialog box with details of the font style, size and attributes required.

③ Click **OK**.

• In Access the whole table is formatted; in Works the selected field(s) are formatted.

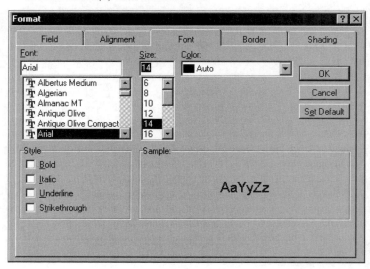

Cell format

You can change the appearance of your cells using border and shading options.

Access

① Choose **Datasheet**... from the **Format** menu.

② Specify which gridlines you wish to show, the gridline colour, the background colour and cell effect required.

③ Click **OK**.

Works

① Select the fields(s) you wish to format.

② From the **Format** menu choose **Border**... or **Shading**...

③ Specify the options required.

④ Click **OK**.

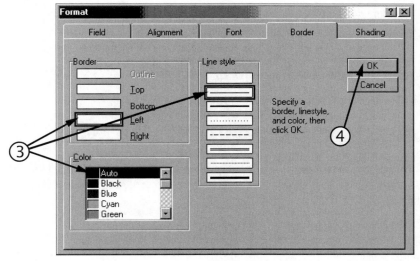

Forms

As an alternative to entering and editing data into a table, you could use a *form*. Forms tend to be more user friendly. You can set up customised form layouts – perhaps to look like a pre-printed form you actually use, e.g. application forms or invoices. Or you can usually get your application to auto-matically generate a simple but effective form.

Access has a useful tool that builds a simple form automatically – AutoForm.

Try it: AutoForm in Access

① Select the table you wish to use from the Tables list in the Database window.

② On the Database toolbar, click the drop-down arrow to the right of the New Object tool.

③ Choose **AutoForm**.

The table you selected is displayed using a simple form layout.

You can move around in Form view in the same way as you did in Datasheet view.

The data you enter or edit in your form in Form view will be stored in the table on which the form is based. Even if you opt not to save the form itself, the data will still be stored in the table.

You can also create an AutoForm from Datasheet view

If you have been working on your table in Datasheet view, you can easily change to Form view using the AutoForm tool.

Try it: Display a form in Works

• Click the Form View tool ▦.

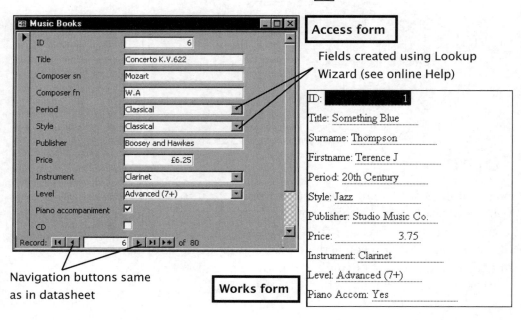

Access form

Fields created using Lookup Wizard (see online Help)

Navigation buttons same as in datasheet

Works form

Find, sort and filter

The *real* power of a database application is demonstrated when you want to find, sort and extract data that you have stored in your tables.

You should be able to:

- Locate records using a Find command.

- Sort records into ascending or descending order – on more than one field if necessary.

- Extract records from your tables that meet specific criteria, e.g. all the jazz or blues music books, or all those by a particular composer.

Try it: Manipulate the data in your table

Access

In Access, you can locate a record using the navigation buttons, or go to a specific record by entering its number in the number field within the navigation buttons.

You can also locate records using **Find**:

① In Datasheet view, click in the field that contains the text you want to find.

② Click the **Find** tool 🔍 on the **Table Datasheet** toolbar.

③ Enter details of what you are looking for in the **Find What** field.

④ Edit the other fields as necessary.

⑤ Click **Find Next** to find the first matching record.

⑥ If it is not the record you want, click **Find Next** until you reach the correct record.

⑦ Close the dialog box once you have found your record.

If Access can't find what you are looking for, a dialog box will appear telling you that the search string wasn't found. If this happens, check your entry in the **Find What** fields carefully – you may have typed it in incorrectly.

Works

① Choose **Find** from the **Edit** menu.

② Enter the text you are looking for and select either **Next record** or **All records**.

③ Click **OK**.

If you select **All records** in the **Find** dialog box, the matching records are extracted – and they alone are then displayed

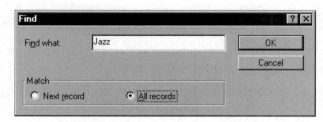

It doesn't matter what field the find text is in, Works will locate it.

'Jazz' found in more than one field

✓		Title	Firstname	Surname	Period	Style
☒	1	Something Blue	Terence J	Thompson	20th Century	Jazz
☒	2	Jazz Technique	Artie	Shaw	20th Century	Scales and Studies
☒	9	Microjazz	Christopher	Norton	20th Century	Jazz
☒	12	Jazzin' About	Pamela	Wedgwood	20th Century	Jazz
☒	16	Jazz Rock and More	Andrew	Wilson	20th Century	Jazz
☒	21	Christmas Jazz	James	Rae	20th Century	Christmas
☒	22	Christmas Jazzin' About	Pamela	Wedgwood	20th Century	Christmas
☒	33	All That Jazz	James	Power	20th Century	Jazz
☒	38	Maiden Voyage	Various	Various	20th Century	Jazz
☒	40	Jazz Playalong for Clarinet	Various	Various	20th Century	Jazz
☒	44	Christmas Jazzin' About	Pamela	Wedgwood	20th Century	Christmas
☒	53	Jazz Pieces Book 1	Various	Various	20th Century	Jazz
☒	57	Jazzin' About	Pamela	Wedgwood	20th Century	Jazz
☒	63	Christmas Jazzin' About	Pamela	Wedgwood	20th Century	Christmas
☒	79	Microjazz Saxophone Duets	Christopher	Norton	20th Century	Jazz
☐	81					

- To display all your records again, open the **Record** menu, select **Show** then click **All Records**.

Another technique that can be used to display a subset of your records in Works is *marking* the records, then requesting the marked records (or unmarked records if you want the opposite) to be displayed.

To mark or unmark a record:

- Click in the box at the left edge of the record. A tick in the box means that the record is marked.

To display marked or unmarked records only:

① Open the **Record** menu.

② Select **Show**.

③ Click **Marked Records** or **Unmarked Records** to display the set you want.

Sort

You can sort records into ascending or descending order. Both alphabetic and numeric data can be sorted. Most applications allow you to sort on more than one field – usually up to three.

Try it: Sort in Access

An ascending or descending sort on one field can be performed at the click of a button in Access.

① Open the table you want to sort in Datasheet view.

② Place the insertion point anywhere within the field you want to sort the records on.

③ Click **Sort Ascending** ⬜ or **Sort Descending** ⬜.

When you close a table that you have sorted, you will be asked if you want to save the changes.

• To save the records in the new, sorted order, choose **Yes**; if you don't want to save the changes, choose **No**.

Multilevel sort

If you want to sort your table on several fields, you must set up your sort requirements in the Filter dialog box. Your table should be displayed in Datasheet view.

① Open the **Records** menu and select **Filter ▶ Advanced Filter/Sort...**

• In the upper half of the **Filter** dialog box, the field list of the current table is displayed. Scroll through the list until you see your main sort field.

② Double-click on the field name – it will appear in the first row, first column of the query grid.

③ Set the sort option in the **Sort** row below the field name.

④ Return to the upper pane and double-click on the field for your second-level sort.

⑤ Click the **Apply Filter** tool ▽ on the **Filter/Sort** toolbar to display your records in the new order.

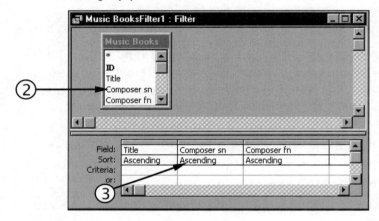

Try it: Sort in Works

① Open the **Record** menu.

② Choose **Sort Records** ...

③ Specify the fields that you want to sort by.

④ Set the sort order – ascending or descending.

⑤ Click **OK**.

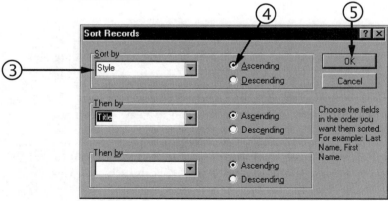

You can sort on up to three fields in the **Sort Records** dialog box.

Filter

You can display those records that meet specific criteria. Your table may have hundreds of records in it, so a feature that can display a selected set is very useful.

This can be done by *filtering* the records. You can filter your records *By Selection* or *By Form* in Access.

Try it: Filter your records By Selection (Access)

① Open the table in Datasheet view if necessary.

② Position the insertion point in the field of a record that has the criteria you are looking for.

③ Click the **Filter By Selection** tool.

A subset of the records within the table will be displayed.

• You can filter your filtered list using the same technique – narrowing down your list of records as you go.

• To display all your records again, click, the **Remove Filter** tool.

Try it: Filter your records By Form (Access)

When you Filter By Form, you can specify multiple criteria at the one time (unlike Filter By Selection where you narrow down your search one criterion at a time).

① Click the **Filter By Form** tool.

You are presented with an empty record. As you move from field to field, you will see that each field behaves like a combo box (drop-down list) in which you can display the options.

② Select the filter criteria using the drop-down lists.

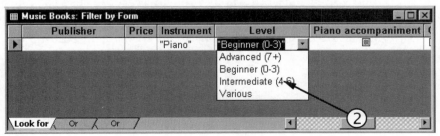

③ Click the **Apply Filter tool**  – all records meeting the criteria specified will be displayed.

④ To display all the records again, click **Remove Filter** .

If you have set up a filter that you might want to reuse, you can save the criteria set from the **Filter By Form** dialog box.

① Click the **Save As Query tool** .

② Give your query a name.

③ Click **OK**.

You will find the query listed in the Database window.

- To apply the filter and display the results from the **Database** window, select it in the Queries list, then click **Open**.

Operators

When you specify criteria in Filter by Form, Access assumes you mean equal to (=). To get a different selection of records you can precede your entry with any of these operators:

Less than	<	Greater than	>
Less than or equal to	<=	More than or equal to	>=
Equal to	=	Not equal to	<>
Between...And...			

Try it: Filter in Works

① Click the **Filter** tool 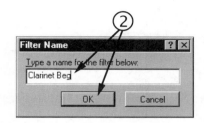.

② Give your filter a name and click **OK**.

③ Enter the criteria.

④ Click **Apply Filter**.

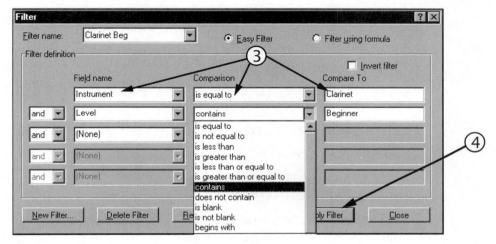

* To show all your records again, open the **Record** menu, select **Show** and click **All Records**.

Once you've created a filter, you are taken directly to the **Filter** dialog box each time you click the **Filter** tool. An existing filter can be selected from the drop-down list.

After selecting a filter:

* To apply it click **Apply Filter**...

* To rename it click **Rename Filter**...

* To delete it click **Delete Filter**...

* If you want to create a new filter, click **New Filter**...

* You can also apply an existing filter from the **Record** menu – choose **Apply Filter**, then click the filter name you wish to apply.

Printing your tables

If you want a paper copy of your data, you can easily print out the contents of your tables.

Try it: Print a table

Access

• Select the table in the Database window and click the **Print** tool.

Or

• Open the table in Datasheet view and click the **Print** tool.

Works

① Display the list of records for the table you wish to print.

② Click the **Print** tool.

Margins and orientation

If you need to change the margins, or the orientation of your table before you print it, you must go into the **Page Setup** options. If you are using Access you should display the table in Datasheet view.

To view the page setup options:

① Open the **File** menu.

② Select **Page Setup**...

③ Specify the setup options.

④ Click **OK**.

• On the **Margins** tab of the dialog box, you can change the top, bottom, left or right margins.

• On the **Page** tab in Access or the **Source, Size & Orientation** tab in Works, you can change the orientation (portrait or landscape), the paper size and source details.

• In Works, on the **Other Options** tab, you can specify whether or not to print gridlines, row and field labels, and set the starting number for page numbers.

Reports

As an alternative to printing out the contents of a table directly from the table, you could specify the layout for your printout by using the application's *report* feature.

In Access, you can quickly design a simple report from any of your tables or queries using **AutoReport**. The report produced is a simple, single column report, listing all the fields in each record of the table or query.

I suggest you also try the **Report Wizard**. Select **Reports** in the **Objects** bar, double-click **Create Report by using a Wizard** and work through the steps.

Try it: Create an AutoReport in Access

① Select the table or query in the Database window.

Or

• Open the table or query to display the list of records.

② Display the **New Object** list.

③ Select **AutoReport**.

• A simple report will be created using the data in the table or query.

④ When you close your report you will be asked if you want to save it. If you do, it will be listed under **Reports** in the **Database** window.

Design view is not discussed here. You can use it to customise many features of a report layout – a well designed report can look so professional that you might think that it has been produced using a word processor or a DTP application.

Key points to note about reports

• Reports are displayed in Print Preview – so you can see what the page would look like if you were to print it out.

• You can use the navigation buttons at the bottom of the Print Preview window to move through the pages.

• Click the **View** tool on the **Print Preview** toolbar to take your report through into Design view.

Try it: Create a report in Works

① Display your table.

② Click the **Report View** tool  on the toolbar.

③ If the **First-time Help** dialog box appears, click **OK**.

④ Give your report a name and click **OK**.

⑤ Work though the steps in the **ReportCreator**, to select the layout and fonts, the fields to include, their order, grouping, etc. and click **Done** when you've finished.

You will be asked whether you wish to view your report in preview, or modify it. Click **Preview** to see the report.

Music Books.wdb - Book List

Title	Firstname	Surname	Price
Blues			
Classic Blues	Various	Various	£9.99
		SUM:	
			£9.99
Christmas			
Christmas Jazz	James	Rae	£5.95
Christmas Jazzin' About	Pamela	Wedgwood	£5.95
Christmas Jazzin' About	Pamela	Wedgwood	£5.95
Christmas Jazzin' About	Pamela	Wedgwood	£5.95
The Snowman	Howard	Blake	£6.95
Violinists' Book of Carols	Various	Various	£1.95
Walking in the Air	Howard	Blake	£3.95
		SUM:	
			£36.65
Classical			
Ballet Highlights	Various	Various	£7.95
Clarinet Quintet K.V.581	W.A	Mozart	£5.50
Concertino	Giuseppe	Tartini	£7.95
Concertino in D Op.15	Ferdinand	Kuchler	£3.95

A panel is displayed down the right side of the report so you can move through the pages and zoom in and out, print the report or return to the report design (click **Cancel** to do this).

Key points to note about reports

• You can create another report, rename, delete or duplicate an existing report from the **Tools** menu.

• If you have several reports set up, you can choose which one you wish to look at from the View menu.

• When you cancel a report preview, you are taken to the report design screen. This is not discussed here – experiment with it or check out the online Help if you want to use it.

8
Presentations

IN THIS CHAPTER:

- Creating a presentation
- Charts and Organization charts
- Tables
- The Clip Gallery
- Masters
- Slide shows
- Printing presentations

In this chapter we discuss presentation graphics. If you have ever been to a conference where the speaker used animated slides on an overhead projector, or to a slick sales presentation with a slide show, then you have probably seen PowerPoint in action. If you are asked to give a talk on any topic, and feel that a slide show would add interest, you could use PowerPoint to help you prepare your material and deliver your presentation.

PowerPoint is a presentation graphics package. You can use PowerPoint to produce:

Slides

Slides are the individual pages of a presentation. They may contain text, graphs, clip art, tables, drawings, animation, video clips, etc. PowerPoint allows you to present your slides via a show on a computer, 35mm slides or overhead projector transparencies.

Notes pages

A speaker's notes page accompanies each slide you create. Each notes page contains a small image of the slide plus any notes you type in. You can print the pages and use them to prompt you during your presentation.

Handouts

Handouts consist of smaller, printed versions of your slides that can be printed 2, 3, 4, 6 or 9 slides to a page. They provide useful backup material for your audience and can easily be customised with your logo or company name.

Outline

Your presentation Outline contains the slide titles and main text items. The Outline gives a useful overview of your presentation's structure.

PowerPoint objects

The text and graphics that you can place on a slide in PowerPoint are called **objects**. An object may be:

* Text   • Drawing   • Graph   • ClipArt   • Movie
* Organization Chart   • Table   • WordArt   • Sound

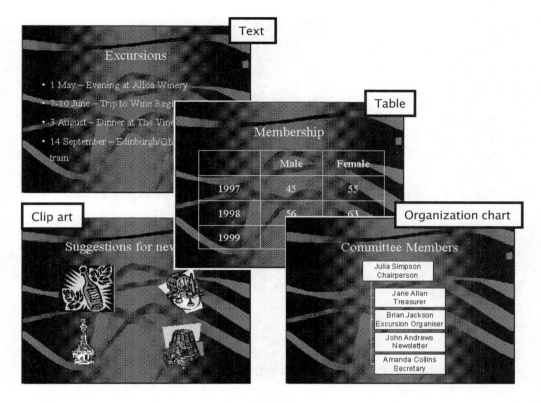

Creating a presentation

Getting started

When you open PowerPoint you arrive at the PowerPoint dialog box. You will probably start most of your presentations from this point. The options for creating a new presentation are:

- **AutoContent Wizard** – Use this option if you want to start by using a wizard that helps you work out the content and organization of your presentation.

- **Design Template** – This options lets you pick a presentation template with the colour scheme, fonts and other design features already set up.

- **Blank presentation** – If you opt for this one, you get a blank presentation with the colour scheme, font and design features set to the default values.

In this chapter we'll use the Blank presentation option, but you should experiment with the other options and use whichever method you prefer

To create a new blank presentation from within PowerPoint, click on the Standard toolbar. Select the slide layout required for the first slide from the **New Slide** dialog box and click **OK**

You can also choose:

• **Open an existing presentation.** which takes you to the **Open** dialog box.

Try it: Create a new presentation

① At the **PowerPoint dialog box** select the **Blank presentation** option.

② Click **OK**.

③ Choose a slide layout for your first slide – usually the Title Slide.

④ Click **OK**.

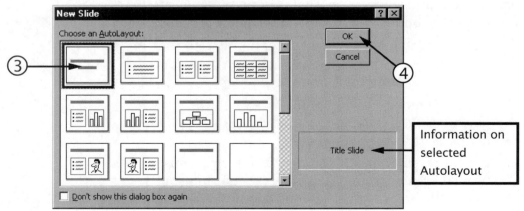

- The boxes with broken outlines that appear when you create a new slide are called placeholders. Different slide layouts have different placeholders set up on them – the placeholders will contain the slide title, slide text and any other objects that you display on your slide.

The PowerPoint window is very similar to other Office application windows.

The Standard and Formatting toolbars usually appear along the top of the window. The Drawing toolbar is usually along the bottom of the window.

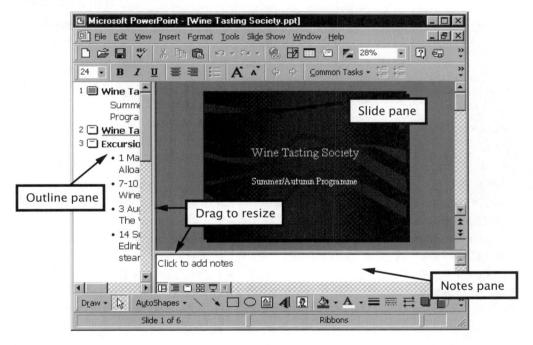

View options

By default, PowerPoint displays all new presentations in Normal view (PowerPoint 2000). You can use the view icons at the bottom left of the screen to get a different view of your presentation.

You will do most of the work setting up your presentation in Normal, Outline or Slide view – it's very much a matter of personal preference.

You can also go into Slide Show view at any time to see how your slide will look in the final presentation. Press [Esc] from Slide Show view to return to your presentation file

The **View** menu has the option **Notes Page view.** This displays a miniature of your slide, with the notes area below (see page 190). If you wish to enter and edit notes in this view use the **Zoom** tool set at 75% so that you can read the text

Key points: view options

- In Normal, Outline and Slide view, you have three panes displaying different parts of your presentation.

- The slide itself is in the top right pane, notes are displayed in the bottom right pane and an outline of your presentation is displayed in the left pane.

- You can resize the panes – click and drag their borders.

- You can also view your presentation in Slide Sorter view and Slide Show view.

- In Slide Sorter view each slide is displayed in miniature – this view can be used for moving slides around and to help you prepare for the actual presentation.

- I suggest you use Normal view for the most part – I think you'll find it the best compromise. Try out the others and see what you think – I prefer Normal.

Working with slides

Once you've created your presentation, the next step is to decide on the text that you want to appear on your slides – the title, and the main points that you want to discuss during your presentation.

The main text on a slide will be in the slide title or the bulleted list area.

You can determine the structure of the text on each slide (main points, sub-points etc), using up to five levels.

Slide Title

Level 1
  Level 2
    Level 3
      Level 4
        Level 5

To enter text onto a new slide, e.g. the title slide created when setting up a presentation, follow the prompts.

Try it: Enter text

① Click in the Title area and key in your title text.

② Click in the bulleted list area.

③ Key in your text and press **[Enter]**.

④ Repeat step 3 until all your points are listed.

You can add new slides at any place in your presentation.

Try it: Add a new slide

① View the slide that you want *above* your new one.

② Click the **New Slide** tool 🖻 (*not* the **New** tool).

③ Select a layout and click **OK**.

In the slide pane, you can see one slide at a time. If you have several slides, move up or down through them to view them.

Try it: Move between slides

① Drag the elevator up or down the scroll bar to the slide.

Or

② Click the **Previous Slide** button to move up a slide.

③ Click the **Next Slide** button to move down a slide.

If you have created a presentation using the AutoContent Wizard, select the text on each slide and replace it with your text

You can move between slides with **[Page Up]** and **[Page Down]**

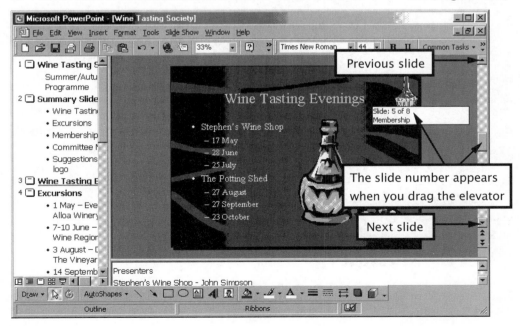

To increase or decrease the paragraph spacing select the paragraphs then click 〖≣〗 or 〖≣〗 on the Formatting toolbar

Try it: Edit text

① Click to place the insertion point in the text to be edited.

② Insert or delete characters as required.

• Or select the old text and key in the replacement text.

Structuring the text on your slide

The points you make on a slide can be structured – you may have main points (at the first bulleted level) and sub-points (at the second, third, fourth or even fifth level).

Initially, all points on your slide are at level 1. You can easily demote sub-items if necessary (and promote them again if you change your mind).

① Place the insertion point in the item.

Most formatting options, e.g. bold, alignment, bullets, etc. work in the same way as in other applications

To demote an item:

② Click the **Demote** tool 〖➡〗 on the Formatting toolbar.

To promote an item:

③ Click the **Promote** tool 〖⬅〗.

Try it: Move bullet points

You can rearrange the points using cut and paste or drag and drop techniques, *or* click inside the item and press **[Shift]-[Alt]-[⬆]** to move it up, **[Shift]-[Alt]-[⬇]** to move it down.

Try it: Move slides

① Go into **Slide Sorter view**.

② **Drag and drop** the slide miniatures to move the slides.

Try it: Deleting slides

To delete a slide in the slide pane, choose **Delete Slide** from the **Edit** menu

① In the **Outline** pane (in Outline or Normal view), click the slide icon on the left of the title to select the slide.

② Press the [Delete] key on your keyboard.

Layout

If you change your mind about the layout you want for a slide, you can easily change it.

Try it: Change the slide layout

① View the slide whose layout you wish to change.

② Click the **Slide Layout** tool 🖼 on the **Standard** toolbar.

③ Select the layout you wish to use and click **Apply**.

Changing the template

You can change your presentation template at any time. The template determines the design elements of your presentation – colour, fonts, alignment of text etc. When you create a presentation using the Blank presentation option the default design template is used.

Try it: changing the template

① Double-click the template name field on the Status Bar.

If you want to add slide numbers, the date, time or any other header or footer to your slide, notes or handouts use the Header and Footer command – it's in the View menu. You have the option of applying your selection to the current slide or to all slides

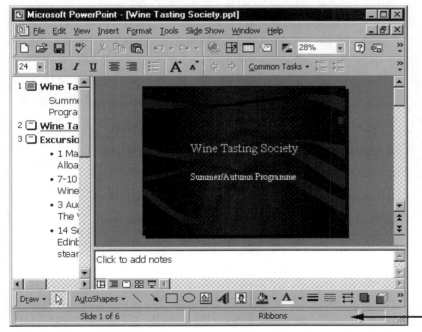

Or

• Choose **Apply Design Template**... from the **Common Tasks** list.

② Select the Template you want to use and click **Apply**.

Charts

Charts (graphs) can be useful if you have figures to present but feel that a graphical representation would be more effective than the figures themselves. They're easy to create, can be very effective (and are good fun to do!).

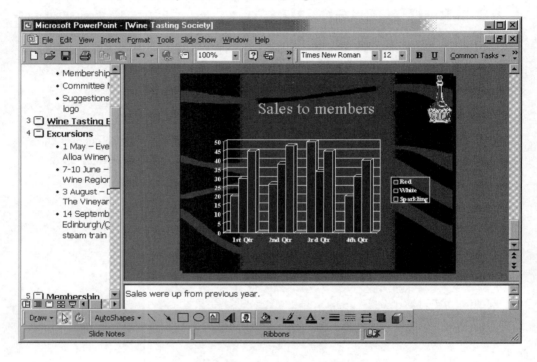

Try it: creating a chart on a slide

① Create a slide that has a **Chart** placeholder.

② Double-click within the placeholder to create your chart.

Datasheet and toolbars

Some new tools will appear on the Standard and Formatting toolbars – these tools can be used to help format your chart.

There is also a small Datasheet window (which can be moved or resized as necessary), where you can key in the data you want to chart.

Entering your own data

The datasheet contains sample data – you must replace this with your own. If you do not need to replace all of it, delete the data that is not required – select the cells and press [Delete].

① Select the cell into which you wish to enter data.

② Key in the data.

③ Move to the next cell you want to work on – use any of the methods shown below.

Key points: Moving around your datasheet

To move from cell to cell you can use:

Arrow keys to move one cell in the direction of the arrow

[Tab] to move forward to the next cell

[Shift]-[Tab] to move back to the previous cell

[Enter] to move down to the next cell in a column

Or

• Point to the cell and click on a cell to select it.

Once you have keyed in your data, you can Hide the datasheet so you can see the chart clearly. You can view it again if you need to edit any data. Click the **View Datasheet** tool to view or hide the Datasheet

By Row and By Column

The Category axis has labels taken from the column or row headings in the datasheet. Use the **By Row** or **By Column** tools on the Standard toolbar to indicate whether your data series is in rows or columns. A graphic in the row or column heading of your datasheet indicates the selected option.

Chart type

The default chart type is a column chart. You can try out a variety of others using the **Chart Type** tool on the **Standard** toolbar.

① Click the drop-down arrow to display the chart types.

② Choose one.

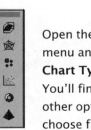

Open the **Chart** menu and choose **Chart Type**... You'll find lots of other options to choose from

Hiding columns

If you don't want all your data to be displayed, you can hide rows or columns as required. This is done on the datasheet.

① Display the datasheet if necessary.

② Double-click on the heading of the column or row.

• The data is dimmed, and is not displayed on your chart.

③ Double-click the heading again to 'unhide' a column or row.

Colours and patterns

Use the Text Box and Arrow tools on the Drawing toolbar to add emphasis to your charts

If you don't like the colour of a data series – the bars representing one set of data on your chart – try experimenting with the options available.

Try it: Change the colour of a data series

① Click on an item (e.g. bar or line) in the data series.

② Click the **Fill Color** down arrow on the Drawing toolbar.

③ Select a colour.

Or

• Click **Fill Effects** to open a dialog box with more options.

④ Experiment with the options to find something you like.

⑤ Click **OK**.

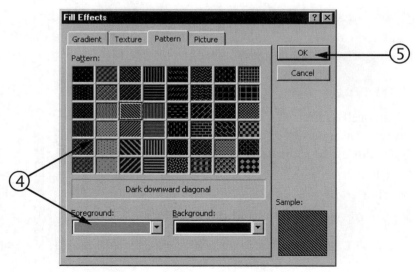

To change the colour of an individual entry in a data series:

① With the chart selected, click on an item (e.g. bar or line) in the data series – this will select the whole series.

② Double-click on the individual entry that you wish to edit.

③ Select the options and click **OK**.

Try it: Format chart objects, e.g. data series, chart title, gridlines, legend or axes

① Double-click on the object you wish to format.

② Select the options required from the **Format** dialog box.

③ Click **OK**.

If you wish to edit a chart that is on a slide, simply double-click on it

Return to your presentation

When your chart is complete, click anywhere on the slide outside the chart placeholder to return to your presentation.

Organization charts

Organization charts offer another way to make your point with a diagram rather than words. This section introduces Microsoft Organization Chart and some of its features. If you use a lot of organization charts, tour through its menus and the on-line Help to appreciate its full potential.

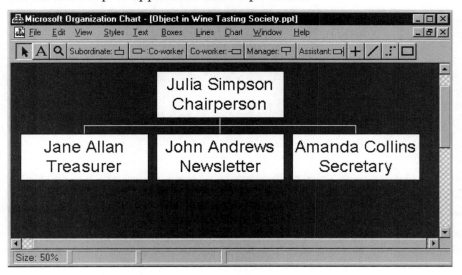

Try it: Create an organization chart

① Create a new slide with an organization chart placeholder on it.

② Double-click within the chart placeholder on your slide.

Key points on organization charts

• Keep them simple – don't have too many boxes – remember that they'll be displayed on a screen or overhead.

• Make them easy to read – you don't *have* to use every formatting option just because they're available.

Text and boxes

Work out the structure you wish to display before you start.

Organization charts can be very complicated structures but they have only simple elements. A basic structure is provided for you. You can build your chart up by adding boxes where needed, and deleting any which are no longer required.

Try it: Enter some text

① Click in the box you wish to edit.

② Key in your data and press **[Enter]** or the arrow keys to move to the next row.

③ Click on the next box to be completed, or anywhere outside the box, when you are finished.

There is a small set of tools – most are for adding boxes, and all the normal range of relationships are covered.

To delete a box, click on it to select it then press **[Delete]**

Try it: Add a box

① Select the box type from the Toolbar – click on it.

② Click on the box to which the new box is related.

[Ctrl]-[D] toggles the display of the drawing tools on the toolbar

Text and drawing tools

The text and drawing tools can be used to add the finishing touches to your organization chart. If you need text outside the boxes on your chart, use the **Text** tool.

Try it: Use the text tool

① Click the **Text** tool A.

② Click to position the insertion point and key in the text.

③ Click anywhere outside the text area when you've done.

The Drawing tools

There are four drawing tools – three types of line and a box.

Try it: Use the drawing tools

① Select a tool.

② Click and drag to draw the line or box.

Chart title

You can enter a title into the chart itself or in the Slide Title placeholder on your slide. If you opt to key in the title in the Slide Title placeholder, delete the *Chart Title* prompt.

• Select the *Chart Title* prompt and either key in the title or press [**Delete**] to remove it.

Key points: zoom options

You can zoom in and out on your chart to get a closer look at what's there, or to get an overview. There are four options:

[**F9**] Size to Window – for an overview of the whole chart.

[**F10**] 50% of Actual – the best mode for normal work.

[**F11**] Actual Size (100%) – in this mode the Zoom tool toggles to Size to Window.

[**F12**] 200% of Actual – if you want to get really close.

Finishing touches

Use the **Styles**, **Text**, **Boxes** and **Lines** menus to add the finishing touches to your organization chart – edit the line styles, add shadows to the boxes, change the colour, size and font of text, etc. Experiment with the options.

To select several boxes or lines at once, select one, hold [**Shift**], and click on the others

① Select the box(es) or line(s).

② Experiment with the options in the menus.

Return to your presentation

To take your chart back into Microsoft Organization Chart for editing, double-click on it

Once you've completed your chart, you'll need to update the slide and return to the presentation to continue work on it.

① Click the **Close** button on the Microsoft Organization Chart window title bar.

② Click **Yes** at the prompt to update your presentation and return to it.

Tables

If you are accustomed to creating tables using Word, you'll find it very easy to create tables on your slides.

Try it: Create a table on a slide

① Create a new slide with a table placeholder set up.

② Double-click on the table placeholder.

③ Specify the number of rows and columns you need.

④ Click **OK**.

• Complete your table as required.

The Tables and Borders toolbar will appear when a table is selected. Use the tools on it to help you format your table attractively.

• If the toolbar doesn't appear, click the **Tables and Borders** tool 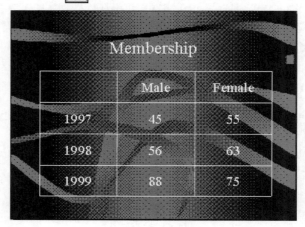 on the **Standard** toolbar to display it.

Click outside the table when you've finished.
Click on your table again if you wish to edit it

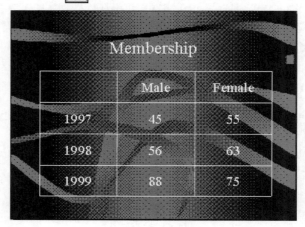

Key points: moving around a table

- Press **[Tab]** to move to the next cell.
- Press **[Shift]-[Tab]** to go to the previous cell.
- Use the arrow keys to move up, down, right and left.
- Click in the cell you wish to work on.

The Clip Gallery

PowerPoint comes with hundreds of Clipart pictures that can be added to your slides, and you'll find that you can access many more on the Internet.

Try it: Create a slide with Clipart on it

① Set up a New Slide with a Clipart placeholder on it.

② **Double-click** within the Clipart placeholder.

③ Select a piece of Clipart.

④ Click **Insert clip**.

Masters

The slides, notes pages and handouts in your presentation all have a *master* or pattern on which they are based. If you want to change something on each slide, e.g. the font or logo, or switch headers or footers on or off, you can do so by editing the master (rather than the individual slide or notes page). Any changes made to a master will be reflected in every slide, notes page or handout based on that master.

There are two masters for your slides – the *title* slide master and the *slide* master.

Slide Master

The Slide Master holds the formatted placeholders for the slide title and text. Changes to the Slide Master will be reflected in every slide in your presentation (except the Title Slide). Any slides where you have made changes to the text formatting at slide level will be treated as exceptions and will retain the custom formatting you applied to them.

Any objects you want to appear on every slide (like your company name or logo) should be added to the Slide Master.

① Choose **Master** from the **View** menu.

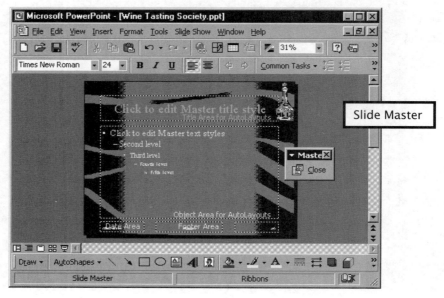

② Select **Slide Master**.

③ Amend the Slide Master as required (using the same techniques you use on a slide in your presentation).

④ Choose an alternative view to leave your Slide Master.

Title Master

You can view and edit the Title Master if you wish. Changes made to the Title Master will only affect the title slide.

① Choose **Master** from the **View** menu.

② Select **Title Master**.

③ Amend the Title Master as required.

④ Choose an alternative view to leave your Title Master.

From any slide except the Title Slide, hold down **[Shift]** and click the **Slide View** button to display the Slide Master – do this on the Title Slide to display the Title Master

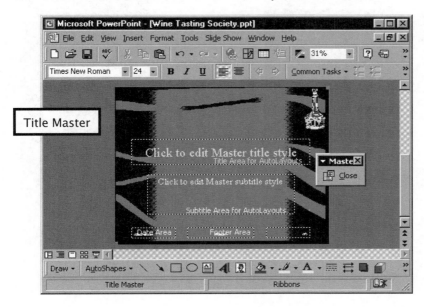

If you have no title slide in your presentation you can easily add one (if you have used the Blank Presentation option you'll have no master title):

① View the **Slide Master**.

② Open the **Insert** menu.

③ Choose **New Title Master**.

Handout/Notes Master

You can also edit the Handout or Notes Master. Anything you add or remove from this will affect each page that you print.

① Choose **Master** from the **View** menu.

② Select **Handout Master** or **Notes Master**.

③ Edit the Master as required.

④ Choose an alternative view to leave your Master.

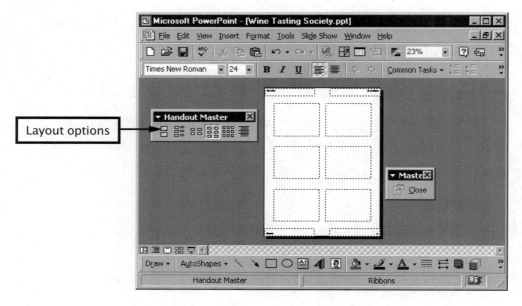

Layout options

The placeholders

The Date, Page Number, Header or Footer placeholders that are on all masters are optional. They can easily be deleted – or put back again if you decide you want them after all.

Deleting placeholders:

① Select the placeholder and press [Delete].

Restoring placeholders:

① In a Master Layout view, select **Master Layout**... (the option depends on the Master) from the **Common Tasks**.

② Select the placeholders.

③ Click **OK**.

Slide shows

Eventually, your slides will be presented in a slide show. There are several features that can be used to help you prepare for the presentation itself, and these are discussed here. I suggest that you work in Slide Sorter view for this section.

Slide Sorter view

Click the **Slide Sorter View** tool ▦ to go into Slide Sorter view. There are several useful features worth exploring in this view, including:

- Hiding slides
- Animating text on slides
- Setting up transitions
- Rehearsing timings

Slide Sorter toolbar

Slide Transition Effects, Preset Animation and Hide Slide can be set in any view using the Tools menu, but I find it easiest to do them from Slide Sorter view using its toolbar.

Hide Slide

This option can prove useful if you're not sure whether or not you will really need a particular slide for your presentation. You can include the slide in your presentation (in case it's needed), but hide it. The hidden slide will be bypassed during your slide show, unless you decide you need to use it.

Try it: Hide a slide

① Select the slide you want to hide.

② Click the **Hide Slide** tool ▣ .

- The number is crossed out under the slide.

- If you want to show the hidden slide during a presentation press **[H]** at the slide preceding the hidden one.

- To remove the hidden status from a slide, select it and click the **Hide Slide** tool again.

Transitions

Use the Slide Show view together with Slide Sorter view when experimenting with animation options. Then you can check that the options you choose are having the desired effect

A transition is an effect used between slides in a show. The default option is that **No Transition** is set, but there are several interesting alternatives that you might find effective for your presentation. The transition effect occurs as the slide that has the effect applied to it *appears* in your presentation.

Try it: Set a transition

① Select the slide to which you wish to add a transition effect.

② Click the **Slide Transition** tool 🗗 .

③ Select the **Effect** from the drop-down list.

④ The **Preview** window demonstrates the effect – click on it to see the effect again.

⑤ Set the **Speed** to **Fast**. Focus your audience's attention on your slides, not the transition method!

⑥ Choose an **Advance** option.

⑦ Add a sound if wanted.

⑧ Click **Apply** or **Apply to All** if you want the effect added to all your slides.

If a transition is set, an icon 🗗 appears below the slide in Slide Sorter view. Click on it to see the transition, or select the slide, then click the Animation Preview tool 🔯

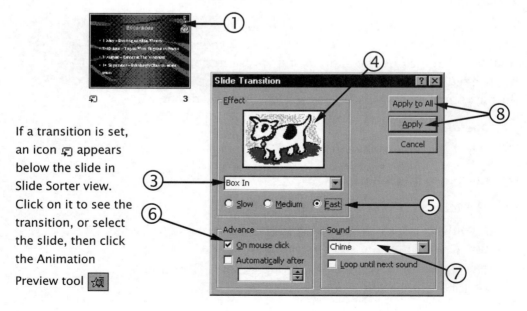

Preset animations

If you have several points listed in the body text of your slide, you could try building the slide up during the presentation, rather than presenting the whole list at once. Experiment with the Preset Animation effects until you find the ones you prefer. You can have a lot of fun messing about with these – but try to avoid having a different effect on each slide!

Try it: Animate a slide

① Select the slide you wish to animate.

② Drop down the **Preset Animation list** on the Slide Sorter toolbar.

③ Choose an effect.

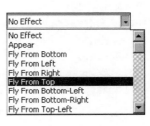

Rehearse timings

It is a good idea to practise your presentation before you go in front of an audience. As well as practising what you intend to say (probably with the aid of notes you have made using the Notes Pages), you can rehearse the timings for each slide.

Try it: Rehearse your timing

① Click the **Rehearse Timings** tool 🔄 .

② Go over what you intend to say while the slide is displayed.

③ Click the left mouse button to build up animated effects (if they are set) or to move to the next slide when ready.

④ Repeat steps 2 and 3 until you reach the end of your presentation.

A dialog box displays the total length of time your presentation took and asks if you want to record and use the new slide timings in a slide show.

You can rehearse your timings as often as is necessary, until you've got the pace right to get your message across

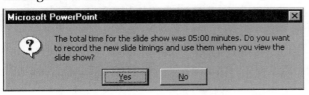

With your slide selected in Slide Sorter view, click the **Slide Show** icon. Click to build up the animated text on the slides and to move through them. Press **[Esc]** at any time to return to the previous view.

- Choose **Yes**, if you want each slide to advance automatically after the allocated time. The slide timings will be displayed in Slide Sorter view.

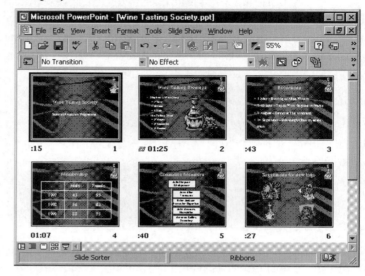

Summary Slide

You can get PowerPoint to automatically produce a Summary Slide for your presentation. PowerPoint takes the title of each slide you select and lists it on the Summary Slide which is placed in front of the first slide that you selected.

Try it: Create a Summary Slide

① Select the slides from which you wish to produce a Summary Slide.

② Click the **Summary Slide** on the Slide Sorter toolbar.

PowerPoint will create as many Summary Slides as is necessary to list the titles from all the selected slides

Key points: selecting slides

- To select one slide – click on it.

- To select several consecutive slides – click on the first slide, **[Shift]-click** on the last one.

- To select non-consecutive slides – click on the first one, hold down **[Ctrl]**, click on each of the other slides.

Running a slide show

You can run your slide show at any time to check how your presentation is progressing. Each slide fills the whole of your computer screen. After the last slide, you are returned to the view you were in when you clicked the **Slide Show** tool.

Try it: Present a slide show

① Select the slide you want to start from, usually the first.

② Click the **Slide Show** icon to the left of the horizontal scroll bar.

③ Press **[Page Down]** or **[Enter]** (or click) to move onto the next slide (or build up animated effects if they are set).

• Press **[Page Up]** to go to the previous slide if necessary.

Slide Show options

When presenting your slide show, you might want to leave the normal sequence, go directly to a slide, or draw on a slide to focus attention. These, and other features, can be accessed using the pop-up menu or the keyboard.

You can exit your slide show at any time by pressing the **[Esc]** key on your keyboard.

Try it: Use the Slide Show options

① Click the right mouse button or the pop-up menu icon at the bottom left corner of the screen.

To go directly to a slide:

② Select **Go**, then **By Title** and choose the slide to go to.

To 'draw' on your screen:

① Press **[Ctrl]-[P]** to change the mouse pointer to a pen.

② Click and drag to draw.

③ Press **[Ctrl]-[A]** to change the pointer back to an arrow when you've finished.

To erase your drawing:

① Press **[E]** on your keyboard.

To get more help on the options available to you while running Slide Show, press [F1]. The Slide Show Help dialog box lists other options you might want to experiment with.

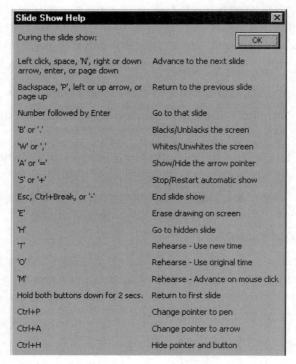

Printing presentations

You can print your whole presentation in PowerPoint – the slides, speaker's notes pages, audience handouts and the presentation outline.

The first stage to printing is to set up the format.

Try it: Set up the format for printing

① Choose **Page Setup** from the **File** menu.

② Select the size from the **Slides sized for** field.

③ Specify the orientation for the **Slides**.

④ Specify the orientation for the **Notes, handouts & outline**.

⑤ Click **OK**.

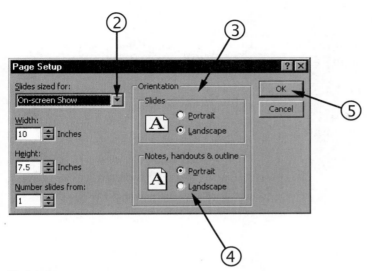

If you change the slide orientation, you may find that you need to change the size and shape of placeholders on the Slide Master to get your objects to fit well

Printing

With the Page Setup details specified to give the output required, you can go ahead and print.

Try it: Print

① Open the **File** menu and choose **Print**.

② In the **Print range** options, specify the slides you want to print.

③ Select Slides, Handouts, Notes or Outline in the **Print what**: list.

④ Click **OK**.

Key points: Print what?

Slides

Prints your slides on paper or overhead transparencies, one slide per page.

Handouts

Prints miniatures of the slides 2, 3, 4, 6 or 9 to the page. Printing your handouts with 3 slides to the page is particularly useful as there is room for your audience to make their own notes.

If you click the **Print** icon on the standard toolbar, one copy of each slide is printed. To print anything else you must access the **Print** dialog box and specify what you want to print in the **Print what:** field

Notes Pages

A slide miniature is printed, together with any notes that you have made to prompt you during your presentation.

Outline View

The text of each slide is printed out, showing the structure of the presentation.

9
Desktop Publishing

IN THIS CHAPTER:

- Introduction to DTP
- Creating a publication
- Specifying your own designs
- Text frames
- Working with objects
- Sidebars and pull quotes

This chapter introduces desktop publishing (DTP). After an introduction to its uses and specialist terminology, we go on to create a DTP file using Microsoft Publisher. Sophisticated word processing applications, e.g. Word have many DTP features, but generally speaking it is easier to get the layout required using true DTP software. This chapter should give you an idea of what DTP is all about.

Introduction to DTP

What can I do with a DTP package?

This chapter assumes you are using Microsoft Publisher, but features similar to those discussed here will be available on most DTP packages

Most DTP packages are easy to use and great fun! You can use DTP to create:

- Newsletters
- Invitations
- Brochures
- Booklets
- Flyers
- Web pages
- Forms
- Cards
- Certificates

– the list goes on and on!

Microsoft Publisher is probably the most popular DTP package for the home or small business user. Professionals would probably use a more sophisticated package, e.g. Pagemaker. A DTP package gives you the tools you need to create your own professional-looking publications – so you may be able to produce many of your own publications without the services of a professional designer!

However, to get the best results from any DTP software you have to start to think like a designer yourself.

Keywords for successful publications:

Simplicity   Consistency   Contrast

With a package like Publisher there are several PageWizard design assistants that can help you create your publication. The wizard does most of the work for you – all you need to add is your own text and pictures. It's the easiest way to start!

Terminology

As you work with DTP software, you'll become familiar with the specialised terminology it uses. Brief definitions of some of the main words and phrases are listed here.

Objects

Text, a picture, table, drawing or anything else that you place on a page is called an object. Try not to have too many objects on any one page – it will give a cluttered effect.

Each object on a page is placed within a *frame*.

Text frames

The text that you type into your publication is entered into a text frame. The edges of the frame work like margins do in a word processing file – text will wrap within the frame. If the text you enter into a frame is more than the frame can accommodate you will have to consider how you can make it fit. You could reword your article (so that it takes up less space), increase the size of the frame or link the text frame to another text frame so that the text will flow from one frame to another.

Picture frames

Pictures – Clipart, logos, or other images – are placed within picture frames in your publication.

Page layout

The layout of a page is very important. You determine the page layout by deciding where you want your text and pictures to go and what size the frames should be.

Text and pictures on foreground

Foreground

Text, pictures, tables, etc. that make up the articles in your publication are placed on the page foreground.

Background

Page numbers, headers, footers or any objects that you want to be repeated on each page of your publication are entered onto the page background. The background is similar in concept to header and footer areas in a word processing package.

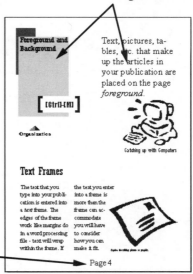

Page numbering on background

White space

Don't be tempted to crowd too much information onto a page (unless the publication is meant for a specialist group who will appreciate it).

White space is the term given to the blank areas on a page. The white space can be in the margins or between items on your page. Effective use of white space can have a positive effect – don't try to fill up every last bit of the page!

Font (Typeface)

You can vary the font, font size or font attributes (bold, italic, etc.) used on a page to draw attention to your text – but don't overdo it.

Margins

A margin is the white space between the edge of the page and the area that your objects are placed within.

Columns and rows

The information on your page will be displayed in columns and rows. You can specify the number of columns and rows you wish to have on each page.

Boundaries and guides

Boundaries and guides are non-printing lines that can be displayed on the screen to show where the margins, column and row boundaries, and edges of frames are. They can be very useful in helping you to position objects on the page.

Design tips

Before you start to set up your publication, give some thought to its design. There are no hard and fast rules when it comes to design, but you want to end up with a publication that gets your message across to your target audience.

Collect ideas

- Look at some similar publications – get an idea of what you think does and doesn't work.
- Use the designs in your application.
- Sketch your ideas out on paper.
- Ask friends for their comments.

Remember the three basic rules

- Keep it simple.
- Be consistent.
- Use contrast to draw attention to your message.

Watch your budget!

Check the paper, printing and binding costs before finalising your design. You may want to change things if it is going to work out too expensive.

Paper – things that might affect your choice

- Printing and copying methods. Some papers are made specifically for commercial printing. Others are ideal for photocopiers and laser printers. Some papers are more suitable for inkjet printing.
- Cost! Some types of paper are much more expensive than others. Your budget will usually narrow down the range of papers available to you – considerably.
- Type of publication. A newsletter or magazine with high-quality colour photographs will look better on a glossy coated paper than on an uncoated one.
- Function and shelf life of publication.

We had a blast...

Colour

Colour can add emphasis to your publication.

Full colour – You have access to up to 16 million colours when using full colour. The main limiting factor in the number and sharpness of colours is the printer you are using. You can print a full colour publication on your desktop printer, or send it to a commercial printer.

Spot colour – This allows you to add up to two colours to your publication (in addition to black). It's useful for highlighting areas.

Coloured paper – Cheap, easy and effective!

Creating a publication

To create a new publication from the Catalog dialog box once you're into Publisher, open the **File** menu and choose **New**. The Catalog dialog box will be displayed

When you start Publisher, the Microsoft Publisher Catalog dialog box appears.

The easiest way to start using Publisher is to use one of the designs listed in the Catalog dialog box. These do most of the hard work for you – all you need do is enter your own text and pictures into the layout. You can select a design from the Publications by Wizard or the Publications by Design tab.

Wizards

Try it: Create a publication using a wizard

① At the Catalog dialog box, select a type of publication from the Wizards on the Publications by Wizard tab (or a Design Set from the Publications by Design tab).

② Select a publication from the previews on the right.

③ Click **Start Wizard**.

Wizard questions

You may be asked questions by the wizard. The steps that the wizard takes you through vary with the publication type. If you choose a different publication wizard you may be asked different questions. Don't worry – just work through it!

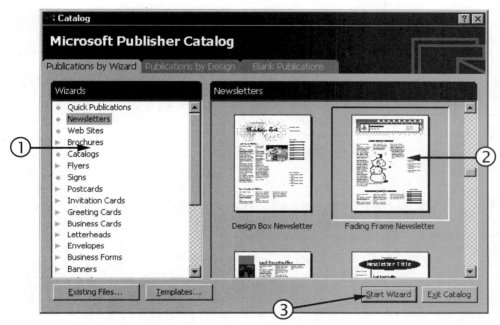

Whether or not the wizard asks questions depends on a set-ting in the **Options** dialog box.

To switch the questions on or off:

① Open the **Tools** menu and choose **Options...**

② Select the **User Assistance** tab.

③ Select or deselect the **Step through wizard questions** checkbox as required.

④ Click **OK**.

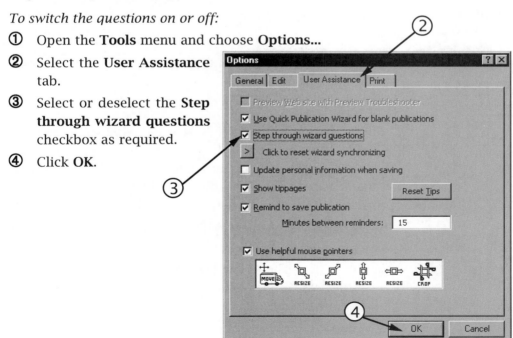

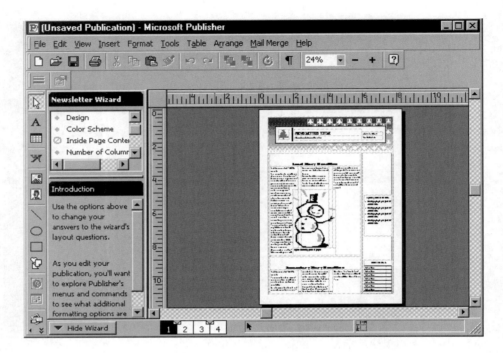

The publication will be displayed, with the Wizard panel on the left

If the Step through wizard questions option is on:

- Click Next > to move on to the next step.
- Click < Back to go back to the previous step.
- Click Finish when you've worked through all the steps.

Wizard panel

You can change several areas of your publication from the Wizard panel. Simply select a category in the top pane, then make the changes required in the lower pane. The options available vary from publication to publication.

You can toggle the display of the Wizard panel by clicking the ▼ Hide Wizard / ∧ Show Wizard buttons at the bottom of the panel.

- In the upper half of the Wizard panel, any option in the wizard with an ⊘ beside it isn't available in the selected publication design.

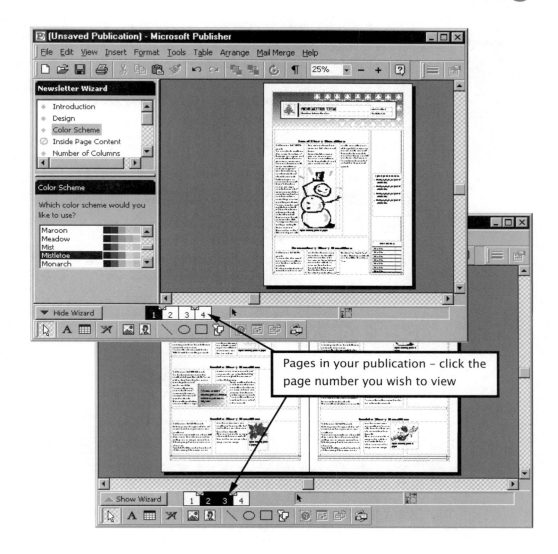

Zooming in and out

You will sometimes want to see a whole page on the screen so that you can get an idea of how it will eventually look. At other times you will want to be able to see part of the publication close up so that you can work on it.

You can easily zoom in and out to get the view you require. Initially, a new publication will be displayed showing a whole page on the screen.

Press **[F9]** to zoom in and out between 100% and the last magnification option used

The Zoom In and Zoom Out tools take you up and down through the magnification options in the zoom list

Try it: Zoom in and out

- Click the **Zoom In** tool + on the Standard toolbar until you reach the magnification required.

- Click the **Zoom Out** tool – to zoom out again.

Or

- Click the drop-down arrow to the right of the Zoom tool 25% ▾ and select the magnification percentage.

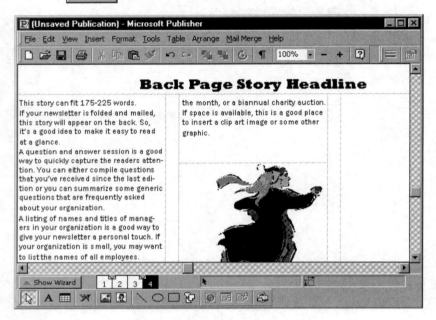

Completing the publication

Having worked through the wizard, check the publication and replace any default, filler text with your own information.

Try it: Complete your publication

① Click the frame you wish to work on.

② Zoom in until you can see the detail.

③ Delete any filler text.

④ Type in your own text.

⑤ Zoom out again.

When you click in a frame filled with filler text, all the text is selected. When you click in a frame where you've entered your own text, the insertion point is placed where you click (so you can edit if necessary).

Frames can be resized. When a frame is selected, black 'handles' appear in each corner and along each side.

Try it: Resize a frame

① Position the mouse pointer over one of the handles – it becomes a resize mouse pointer.

② Click and drag the handle to change the size of the frame.

The pointer shape depends on which handle it is over

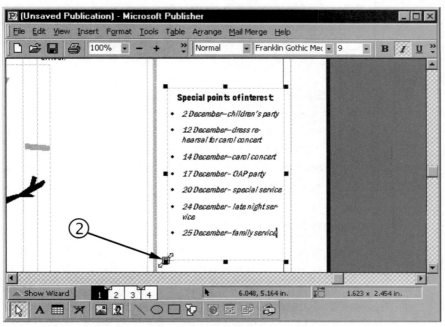

Specifying your own design

Although the designs set up in Publisher are useful, other people will most likely be using them as well, so you may find that your publications look similar to many others you see. You could try designing your own publications to get something totally original!

You can always modify your original plan as you see how the publication develops

Sketch out the design before you start to set it up in Publisher. This will help you think through your ideas and let you decide where you want headings, text, pictures, etc.

Flyer

Here is a possible layout for a flyer, advertising a community event (e.g. BBQ or picnic). It has:

- A large heading;
- Pictures to make it eye-catching;
- An area for important information – date, time and place;
- An area for additional information – attractions, price, etc.

Booklets

If you are designing a booklet, you will have to consider the number of pages. It must be a multiple of 4 - you can set up a 4, 8, 12, 16, etc. page booklet. You should also think about any items that you would want to repeat on each page, e.g. page numbers or headers or footers. These items would be placed on the publication background.

Choosing the page layout

Once you've got some idea about how you want your publication to look, you can start to set it up.

To create a flyer or A4 size poster, select the **Full Page** option. If you are creating a booklet choose **Book Fold**. **Book Fold** publications print pages in groups of four, so you may be prompted to add additional pages if necessary.

Click the **New** tool to quickly create a blank publication using the Full Page option

Try it: Choose a page layout

① Choose **New** from the **File** menu.

② Open the **Blank Publications** tab in the Catalog dialog box.

③ Pick a Blank Publication option down the left of the dialog box - a preview appears on the right.

④ Click **Create**.

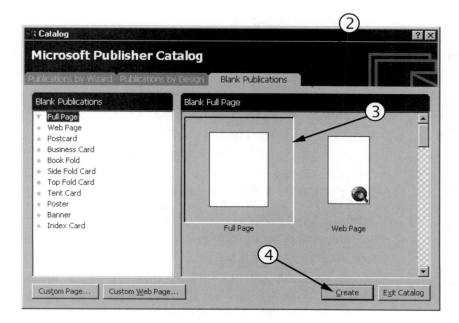

• A new, blank publication will appear on your screen.

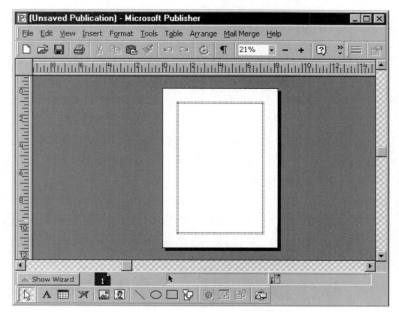

If you want to preview your publication before printing it, you can easily hide the layout guides to give you a clearer view of the page. Press **[Shift]-[Ctrl]-[O]** to toggle the display of the layout guides

Key points: Page Setup

- If you need to change the publication layout, orientation (portrait or landscape) or page size (other than the *Full Page* option) once you've created your publication you can do so in the Page Setup dialog box. The Page Setup command is in the File menu.

- If you are using the Full Page layout and want to change the paper size, open the **File** menu and choose **Print Setup**... You can change the paper size used for full page publications from this dialog box.

Key points: Paper size

- By default, Publisher will print your publication onto A4 size sheets of paper (210 by 297 mm).

- If your publication will be bigger than A4, e.g. a banner or poster, Publisher will print it on a series of A4 sheets, which you can then assemble into the final publication.

Key points: Layout guides

- Layout guides are used to help you position your text and pictures on each page. They do not print out, regardless of whether they are displayed or not.

- There are two main types of layout guides:

  The margin layout guides are pink, and show the position of the top, bottom, left and right margins.

  The grid layout guides are blue, and show the top, bottom, right and left edges of rows and columns.

If you select **Full Page** when creating your publication, the margin and grid layout guides appear together. This is because your page consists of a work area that is one column across and one row high.

Key points: Foreground/Background

Every page has two levels – a foreground and a background.

- The text, heading, pictures, etc. that you want on a page are entered onto the foreground.

- Layout guides and any object that you want to repeat on

every page, such as headers, footers or page numbers must be placed on the background.

- **[Ctrl]-[M]** will take you from foreground to background and from background to foreground.

Rows and columns

In the flyer design drawn up on page 228, the basic page layout consisted of two columns and three rows. To help position the text and graphics accurately on the page, we can add more grid guides to show where the column and row boundaries will be.

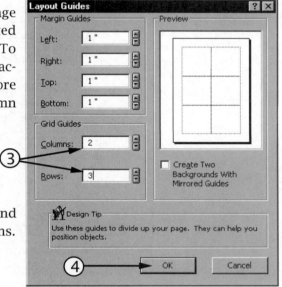

Try it: Add layout guides

① Open the **Arrange** menu.

② Choose **Layout Guides...**

③ Set the number of columns and rows in the **Grid Guides** options.

④ Click **OK**.

Adjusting the guides

The guides split the page up into the number of rows and columns requested. The rows and columns are all the same height and width. If you don't want all your rows and columns the same size, you can easily adjust the position of the guides to make the rows and columns the size you require.

The guides appear on the page background, so you must go there to adjust them.

Try it: Adjust the guides

① Press **[Ctrl]-[M]** to go to the background.

② Hold the [Shift] key down and move the mouse pointer over a guide that you want to move.

- The pointer becomes an ⬍ over a horizontal guide or an ⬌ over a vertical guide.

Check that Snap to Guides is switched on (Tools menu). It's much easier to line things up properly with this option on

③ Keeping the [Shift] key held down, click and drag the guide to move it to its new position.

④ Press **[Ctrl]-[M]** to return to the foreground when you've finished.

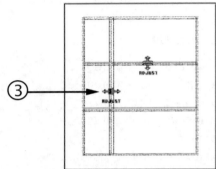

• If you want the guides at a specific place, watch the Object Position indicator 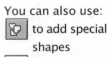 on the Status Bar as you click and drag.

Text frames

Most of the text that you enter onto a page will be placed in a series of text frames on the publication foreground. Text frames are like mini-documents on your page. Text entered into a text frame will wrap between the left and right edge of the frame.

Try it: Insert a text frame

You can also use:
🔲 to add special shapes
🔲 to add Clipart

① Click the **Text Frame** tool 🔲 on the **Objects** toolbar.

② Drag over an area to insert a text frame.

③ Press the **[F9]** key to zoom in on the frame.

④ Type in your text.

⑤ Press **[F9]** again to zoom out when you've finished.

Add as many text frames as you need to your page to help you position your text exactly where you want it.

• For a special text effect you could use a WordArt object – click 🔲 to insert WordArt.

Leading, tracking and kerning

The term *leading* (pronounced 'ledding') is used to describe the amount of spacing between lines of text.

By default, Publisher leaves one space (sp) between lines of text. The size of the space depends on the font size. You can adjust the line spacing from the Line Spacing dialog box (in the Format menu).

Line spacing keyboard shortcuts:

[Ctrl]-[1] sets single spacing

[Ctrl]-[5] sets 1½ spacing

[Ctrl]-[2] sets double spacing.

Tracking

Also known as 'track kerning', this is the adjustment of spacing between *all* characters. You can adjust the tracking to squeeze letters closer together so that they will fit inside a frame or spread the letters out to create a special effect.

Try it: Adjust tracking

① Select the paragraph or text you want to adjust the tracking for.

② Choose **Character Spacing** from the **Format** menu.

③ Specify the tracking options required and click **OK**.

Kerning

Also known as 'letter kerning', this is the adjustment of space between certain pairs of letters in a word. Kerning is used to improve the appearance of specific character pairs that would otherwise appear to be squeezed too closely together, or spread too far apart. Letters with a font size above 14 pt are automatically kerned in Publisher.

To adjust kerning, select the text you want to adjust then choose **Character Spacing** from the **Format** menu. Specify the kerning option required and click **OK**.

Fonts

There are a large number of fonts to choose from in Publisher.

Fonts come in families. If you look down the font list you'll find several from the Arial family, Bookshelf, Eras, Lucida family, etc.

Publisher groups its text fonts into three categories:

- Serif fonts have a little tail (serif) on the straight lines of characters. For large amount of text, use a serif font that's easy to read, e.g. Times New Roman.

- San serif fonts have simpler lines. Their clean, bold appearance makes them useful for headings.

- Script fonts give a hand-written look to your text – attractive on invitations, but some fonts can be difficult to read if used for big blocks of text.

- Publisher's categories are not standard. Fonts are normally divided into serif, sans serif and display - with all the fancier fonts, including scripts, being grouped under display.

Serif fonts	Sans serif fonts	Script fonts
Baskerville Old Face	Arial	*Lucida Handwriting*
Century Schoolbook	Century Gothic	*Monotype Corsiva*
Times New Roman	**Impact**	*Viner Hand ITC*

Working with objects

Text objects do not automatically expand to accommodate the text you enter. If this happened, the arrangement of the objects on your page would change and you might not end up with the effect you desire.

If you want to enter more text into a text frame object than there is room for you could:

- Edit the text so that it fits inside the frame.
- Use a smaller font size.

- Enlarge the frame to fit the text you are entering.
- Use AutoFit to get Publisher to make the text fit.
- Connect to another text frame and let the text flow into it (as described here).

You may need to resize, move, copy or delete an object to get the effect you require. An object must be selected before you can resize, move, copy or delete it – just click within the frame to select it.

① Select the object. The handles appear on the frame.

To resize:

② Point to a handle. The pointer becomes the resizer 🖱. Drag to resize.

To move or copy:

③ Point to the edge. The pointer becomes the mover 🚚. Drag the object to move it.

Or

④ Hold down [Ctrl] and drag to copy it.

To delete objects:

⑤ Right-click on the object.

⑥ Select **Delete Object**.

If you want to move an object by a small amount, you can nudge it into position. Select it, hold down [Alt] and press [←], [→], [↑], or [↓] until it is exactly where you want it. The object will move one pixel (screen dot) at a time

Adding and removing pages

Many of your publications will run to several pages. If you create a publication using the Full Page layout, your file will consist of one page to begin with. If you chose a book fold layout, your file will initially have four pages.

You can add pages at any position within your publication (as long as you're on the foreground).

Try it: adding pages

① Display the page you want to add the new pages beside.

② Open the **Insert** menu.

③ **Choose Page...**

④ Enter the number of pages required.

⑤ Specify where the pages should go.

⑥ Select the **Insert blank pages** option.

⑦ Click **OK**.

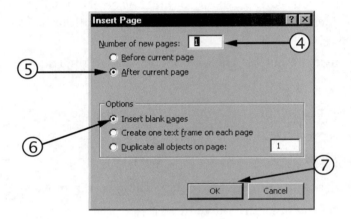

- If you view two pages, e.g. pages 2 and 3, when you access the **Insert Page** dialog box, the options for specifying the position of the new pages are **Before left page**, **After right page** or **Between pages**.

- To delete a page, choose **Delete Page** from the **Edit** menu.

Background objects

Headers, footers and page numbers that you want repeated on every page of your publication are placed within text frames on the background.

Try it: Add background objects

Page numbering:

① Press **[Ctrl]-[M]** to go into Background view

② Create a text frame where you want the page numbering.

③ If you want 'Page', or any other text, to appear before your number, enter it into the text frame.

④ Place the insertion point where you want the number.

⑤ Open the **Insert** menu.

⑥ Choose **Page Numbers**.

⑦ Press **[Ctrl]-[M]** to return to Foreground view.

A # sign will appear on your page background – when you return to the foreground the actual page number will be displayed.

Page header or footer:

① Press **[Ctrl]-[M]** to go into Background view if necessary.

② Create a text frame where you want your page header/footer to go and type in your text.

③ Enter the header and/or footer text.

To insert the current date:

① Choose **Date and Time...** from the **Insert** menu.

② Select the date format.

③ Click **OK**.

④ Press **[Ctrl]-[M]** to return to the foreground.

Sidebars and pull quotes

Text frames can be used to create special effects on a page. You can use a frame to create a sidebar that runs down the side. It is a useful place to put additional information that will be of interest, but is not essential to the understanding of the main text. Try to put your sidebar either on the same page, or within a page or two, of the text it is related to.

Another special effect you can create using a text frame is a pull quote. A pull quote is an excerpt from the main story that adds interest to the page and gets the reader's attention.

You would usually use a larger font for the text in the pull quote (to make it stand out from the rest of the text), and you can also use borders or shading for the same reason.

You can create sidebars and pull quotes from scratch, or use one from the Design Gallery.

Try it: Insert a sidebar or pull quote from the Design Gallery

① Display the page that you want to place a sidebar on.

② Click the **Design Gallery Object** tool .

③ Select **Sidebars or Pull Quotes** in the category list.

④ Choose a design.

⑤ Click **Insert Object**.

⑥ Move or resize the sidebar or pull quote as necessary.

⑦ Click inside the Sidebar – the text becomes selected – and type in your text.

Or

• Click inside the pull quote, delete the dummy text and copy the text required from the main story.

• Click the **Wizard** button at the bottom of the sidebar or pull quote to display the list of options for it. Select an alternative one if you wish.

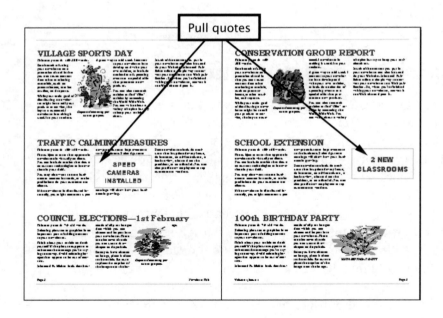

10
Internet and e-mail

IN THIS CHAPTER:

- What you need to get online
- Browsers
- URLs and hyperlinks
- Searching
- Favorites
- E-mail
- Address book
- Sending and receiving messages

This chapter introduces the Internet and e-mail. It give you an idea of what it is all about and will help you get ready to join the online community.

   See 'Catching up with the Internet' for more information on this exciting area.

Getting started

Everyone is talking about it, and the whole world seems to be doing it. What are we talking about? Surfing the Net and communicating via e-mail of course!

If you want to use your PC to get online (rather than your TV, which is another possibility) you'll need:

- your computer;
- a modem (this can be fitted into the processor unit box);
- a telephone socket;
- an Internet Service Provider (ISP), e.g. Freeserve, Demon, AOL or Virgin Net; and
- a browser, e.g. Internet Explorer or Netscape Navigator.

Check out:

- The deals offered by different ISPs – some offer free connection but technical support may be expensive, others have a monthly charge, but give free technical support.
- Whether or not the service provider offers Web space – you might want to set up your own Web page or site!
- Any other services provided by the service provider.
- What friends think of their ISP? Is it a reliable service? What's the support like? Does their system get very busy at times (enough to slow down the rate of access)?
- Companies that offer free trial membership.
- Magazines – they often have free Internet access software on the CDs they carry.

Tips:

- Get a fast modem – they cost more, but will end up cheaper in the long run as your phone bills will be less.
- If your phone socket isn't near your PC, you can get an extension kit and wall-mounted socket to put it within reach – any DIY or PC components shop will have them.
- put your Internet phone number on your 'friends and family' list (if you use BT).

Opening your browser

This chapter assumes that you're using Internet Explorer as your browser, but you'll find that Netscape Navigator is very similar. The first step is opening your browser.

Browser – software that allows you to surf the net

Try it: Open your browser

- Double-click the Internet Explorer shortcut on the Desktop.

Or

① Open the **Start** menu.

② Choose **Programs** and click **Internet Explorer**.

If you have a dial-up connection (one where you connect to your ISP, and through them to the Net, over the public telephone lines) you'll be asked for a user name and password.

The page that appears on your when you open your browser is your home page

③ Complete the dialog box as necessary.

④ Click **Connect**...

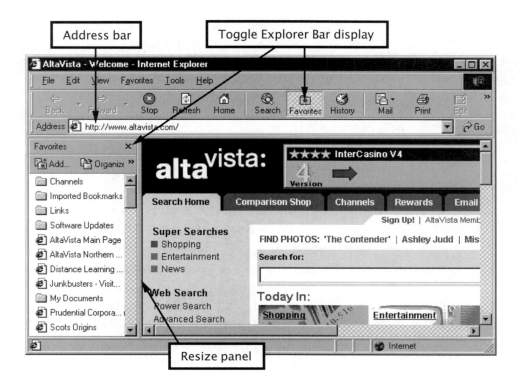

The browser window

Try the Tour in the Help menu – you'll find lots of useful information and tips to help get you started using the Internet

The browser window is similar to that in any other application.

Key points: your browser window

- [F11] toggles the display between Full Screen (without all the toolbars and menu bar) and normal view.
- **Search, Favorites** and **History** toggle the display of a panel, the Explorer Bar, on the left side of the screen.
- The **Explorer Bar** can be resized by dragging its right edge.
- The **Address Bar** displays the URL (see below) of the page you are viewing, or of the one you want to go to.
- The **View** menu options allow you to switch the toolbars (Standard, Address Bar, Links and Radio) on and off.
- The **Status Bar** displays the status of an incoming page.

URLs and hyperlinks

You can visit any page on the Web by entering its URL in the Address bar. A Web page is a screen display that may contain text, graphics, sound, etc. If the information that a company or individual wants to make available on the Web would be better set up on several pages, the pages can be linked together to create a Web site.

URL (Uniform Resource Locator) – the address of a page or other file on the Internet

Key points: URLs

- **http://** identifies a **WWW** (World Wide Web) URL.
- **www** is how WWW addresses usually start (there are exceptions e.g. **http://news.bbc.co.uk**.
- Some URLs are very short e.g. **http://www.coke.com** – this address takes you to the Coke Web site, a commercial organisation based in the USA.
- Some URLs are more complex, e.g. **http://www.orknet. co.uk/lows/index.htm** – this takes you to the home page (**index.htm**) of a company called **Lows**. The site has been set up by a UK company – **orknet.co.uk** tells us that.
- You will find Web addresses everywhere. In newspapers and magazines, on the TV, on items that you buy, etc.

Make a note of any that sound interesting so that you can visit them.

• If you know the URL of a Web page that you wish to visit, simply key it into the Address bar and press [Enter].

You might like to try a visit to some URLs listed here:

http://www.parliament.uk	http://www.lastminute.com
http://news.bbc.co.uk	http://www.cnn.com
http://www.easyjet.co.uk	http://britishairways.co.uk/regional
http://www.ft.com	http://www.askjeeves.co.uk
http://www.scotland.gov.uk	http://www.transformscotland.org.uk
http://www.alton-towers.co.uk	http://www.harryramsdens.co.uk
http://www.thorntons.co.uk	http://www.volkswagen.co.uk
http://www.rbs.co.uk	http://www.virgin.co.uk
http://www.harrods.co.uk	http://www.autotrader.co.uk
http://www.bt.co.uk	http://www.yellowpages.co.uk

Most of these URLs are for companies in the UK (.co.uk), the others are companies in the USA (.com), although some UK companies have .com if they want to reach an international audience, e.g. Financial Times, Lastminute, etc.

Home page

The home page is the one that is displayed when you open your browser application. It is also the one that you are re-turned to when you click [Home] on the toolbar.

You can easily change your home page if you wish – you might want your favourite *search engine* to be your home page, or your own Web page.

Search engine – a system that keeps a database of what's on Web pages and in sites so that you can search for information

Try it: Change the home page
① Locate the page you wish to use for your home page.
② Open the **Tools** menu and choose **Internet Options**...
③ Select the **General** tab.
④ Click **Use Current** within the **Home page** section.
⑤ Click **OK**.

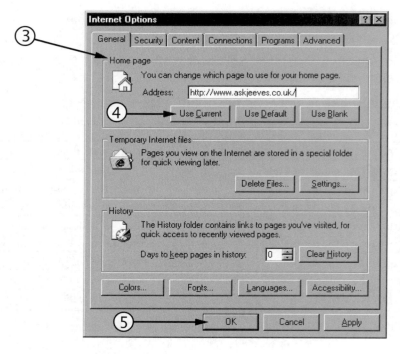

Saving a Web page

If you find a page that you want to be able to view or print when you are not connected to the Internet, you can save it.

① Open the **File** menu.

② Choose **Save As**...

③ Specify the drive/folder that you want the page on.

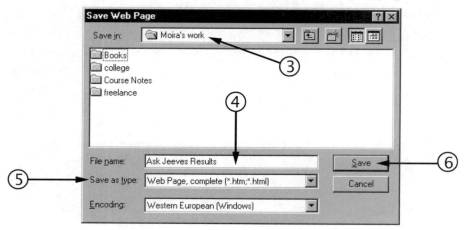

④   Accept or edit the file name.

⑤   Specify the **Save as type** option required.

⑥   Click **Save**.

Working offline

Once you've found a page you want to read, you could disconnect from the Internet while you read it.

Try it: Work offline

①   Restore the ISP dialog box (click on it on the Taskbar).

②   Click **Disconnect**.

If you request a page that is not available offline, you will be prompted to reconnect again.

Hyperlink

Many of the pages that you visit will have hyperlinks to other pages or sites that you may be interested in. A hyperlink is a 'hot spot' that lets you jump from one place on a page to another place on the same page or from one page to another, or to a different site altogether.

Many hyperlinks are text – usually blue with an underline – but they may also be pictures. The pointer becomes a hand with a pointing finger when it is over a hyperlink.

*   To jump to the location that the hyperlink points to, simply click on it.

As you jump from one location to another following hyperlinks, you are *surfing* the Net. As you surf, you may want to revisit pages or sites you have already been to. You could:

*   Click the [Back] and [Forward] tools on the toolbar to move between the pages you've already visited.

Or

*   Click [History] and select the URL of the page you wish to return to.

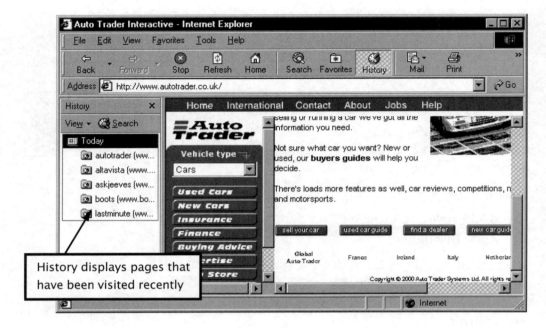

History displays pages that have been visited recently

Searching

If you are looking for information on any topic you can search for. The result of a search is a list of several (sometimes thousands) of pages or sites you may be interested in.

You could perform a search using Explorer's search panel.

Try it: Search in the Explorer Bar

① Click ⊗ Search on the **Standard** toolbar to display the Search panel.

② Choose a category – *Find a Web page* in this case.

③ Enter the word(s) you are searching for – the more details you give, the more appropriate the results will be. For example, to find restaurants in Edinburgh, but not Chinese ones, enter +Edinburgh +Restaurant -Chinese.

④ Click **Search**.

⑤ The Search panel will display a list of sites that you may be interested in. Click on a link to view the page in the main pane of the browser.

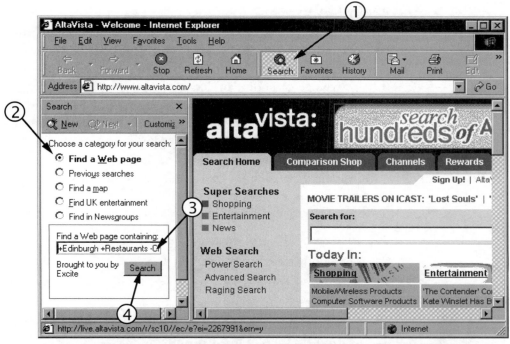

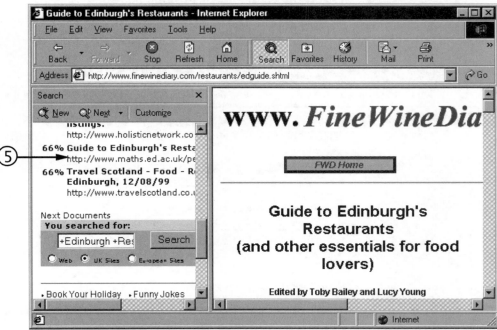

Search engines

Try out a few search engines – they all have a Help facility to help you get started!

Alternatively, you could try some of the many search engines e.g. AskJeeves (http://www.askjeeves.co.uk), AltaVista (http://www.altavista.com), Yahoo! (http://www.yahoo.com), Lycos (http://www.lycos.com) or Excite (http://www.excite.com). The one used in this example is AskJeeves.

Most search engines have a 'directory' to allow you to locate the information you require by working through the various topics – it's down the left of the screen in AskJeeves.

However, if you know what you're looking for it's usually quicker to *search*.

Here I'm trying to find out what's on at my local theatre.

Try it: Search for something

① Type your question in and click **Ask**.

• Jeeves will come back with a list of suggestions to help you refine your search.

② Scroll through the list, and click the **Ask** beside the suggestion that looks most promising.

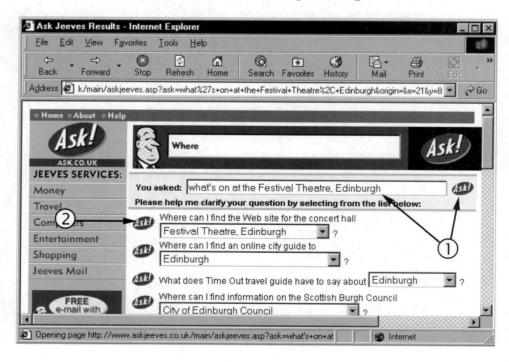

Follow the hyperlinks or explore the site until you find what you're looking for!

Favorites

If you find a site that you know you will want to revisit, you should add it to your list of 'Favorites'. You can then access the site easily without having to enter the URL or search for it again.

Your Favorites list will soon grow! You can set up new folders for them, and rename, move or delete them as necessary.

Try it: Add to your Favorites

① Display the page that you want to add to your list of Favorites.

② Click [Favorites] to display the **Favorites** panel.

③ Click **Add**... at the top of the panel.

④ Edit the page name in the **Name** field if you wish.

⑤   Select the folder that you want to add your page to.

⑥   Click **OK**.

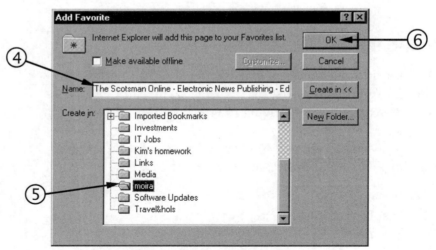

To go to a page in your Favorites list:

①   Display the **Favorites** panel.

②   Open the folder that contains the Favorite.

③   Click on the page required.

Printing

Web pages can be easily printed out. You might want to check/
change the Page Setup options first.

① Open the **File** menu.

② Choose **Page Setup**.

③ Edit the fields as required, e.g. change orientation or page
size, and click **OK**.

④ Click the **Print** tool on the **Standard** toolbar.

Or

⑤ Open the **File** menu and choose **Print**.

⑥ Set the Print options required.

⑦ Click **OK**.

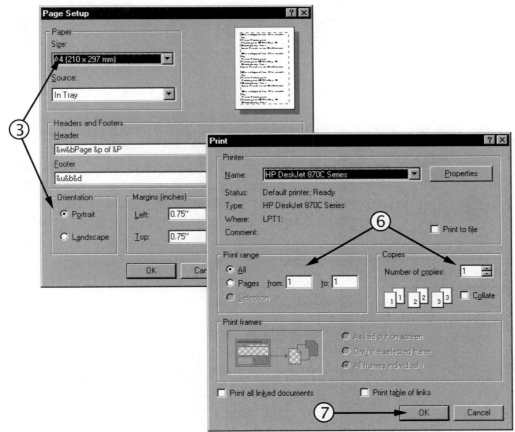

Tips for keeping the cost down

If you are connected to the Internet from home, you will be charged for the time you are online at the same rate as you would be if you were on your telephone. Surfing the Net will result in your phone bill getting bigger (perhaps by quite a bit!). However, you can take a few steps that will help keep your bills down.

- Do your surfing when the rates are at their lowest – in the evening and at the weekend;

- Check out ISPs that give unlimited access options;

- If you use BT, put your ISP number on your Friends and Family list;

- If you find an interesting article you want to read, download the page, then go offline while you read it.

- Alternatively, save the page to your hard drive and read it from there.

E-mail

E-mail – electronic mail

E-mail is quick, cheap and efficient. You can send messages to anywhere in the world for the price of a local phone call. The recipient doesn't need to be at their computer to take your call – the message is just popped in their mailbox and they can collect it when they are ready, day or night.

All e-mail systems provide the same basic facilities. You can:

- Send and receive mail
- Print messages
- Use an Address Book
- Reply to messages
- Delete messages

The following examples use Microsoft Outlook Express.

Opening your e-mail application

① Open Outlook Express from the Start menu in the same way as any other: **Start ▶ Programs ▶ Outlook Express.**

Or

*   Double-click the shortcut on the Desktop.

If you have a dial-up connection (and are not already on-line) the Dial-up Connection dialog box will appear.

② Enter your user name and password, if necessary, and click **Connect**.

Your Inbox will be displayed.

If there is no problem of unauthorised users gaining access to your PC, tick **Save password** so that you don't have to enter it every time.

If your Inbox isn't displayed, click the drop-down arrow to the right of the area identifier in the Folders bar, to display the Folders list, and select **Inbox** from the list

To read a message from your inbox, just double-click on it

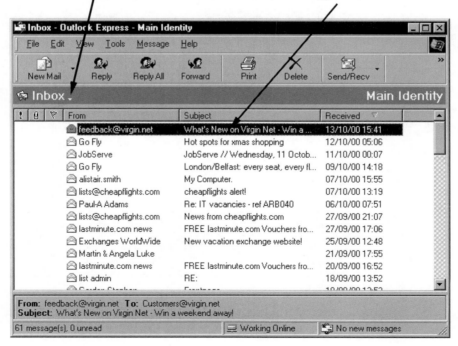

Address Book

As is the case when using traditional methods of communication, i.e. the normal mail service, an address book is a very useful thing. An electronic address book is an integral part of most e-mail applications.

Using the Address Book can save you a lot of time as you don't have to type the addresses into your messages each time you send a message.

Try it: Use the Address Book

①   Open the **Address Book** – click [Addresses] on the toolbar.

To add an address:

②   In the **Address Book**, click **New**, then **New Contact**...

③   Select the **Name** tab in the Properties dialog box.

④   Enter the details.

⑤   Click **OK**.

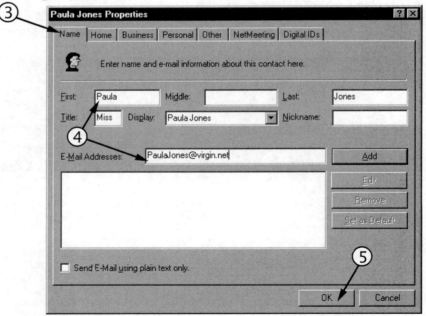

To delete an address:

①   Scroll through the list of names until you see the one you want to delete.

② Select the name – click on it.

③ Click the **Delete** tool or press [Delete].

④ Confirm the deletion at the prompt.

Create and send

It is usually a good idea to work offline when composing your e-mail messages, especially if you're paying for your ISP connection (it helps keep your bills down!).

To disconnect from your ISP

① Restore the ISP dialog box (click on it on the Taskbar) then click **Disconnect**.

Try it: Create and send a new message

① Click 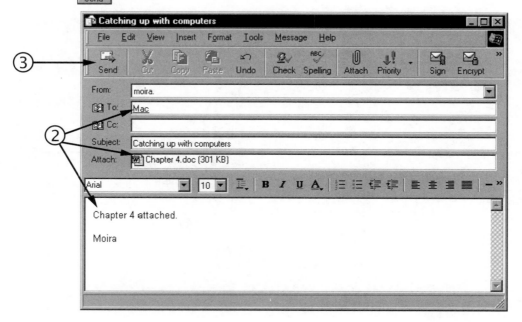 to create a new mail message.

② Complete the **New Message** window (see the notes on the next two pages).

③ Click [Send] when you've finished.

The Outbox is a
holding place for
messages waiting
to be sent

If you're working offline, the message will be placed in your

Outbox, and sent from there when you click .

Notes on using the New Message window

To: and Cc:

The **To:** field is for the main recipient(s);

The **Cc:** field is for those you want to send a copy to;

* Type the address of each recipient into the appropriate field (if there are several addresses, separate them with semi colons ;).

Or

* Click ⊞ To: beside the **To:** field to use the Address Book.

Try it: Complete the fields using the Address Book

① Select the name in the list.

② Click the **To:** or **Cc:** buttons (or **Bcc:** to send a blind carbon copy – only the sender and recipient know who they are if they are in the Bcc list) to add the address.

③ Click **OK**.

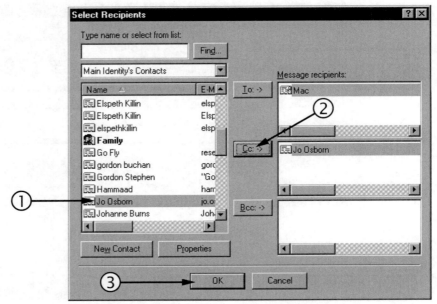

Subject field

Type the message title in the Subject field – this will be displayed in the inbox of the recipient, so they have an idea what the message is about.

Message area

Type your message in here. You can format the text using the formatting tools at the top of the message area if you wish.

Spell check

Spell-check your message before you send it. Click .

Attaching files

You might want to send an existing file to someone – a report or a workbook that you want them to see.

Try it: Attach a file

① Click [📎 Attach] .

② Locate the file that you wish to attach – identify the drive and/or folder in the **Look in** field.

③ Select the file.

④ Click [Attach] .

• Repeat if you have more than one file to attach.

If you attach a file by accident, select it in the **Attach** field and press **[Delete]**

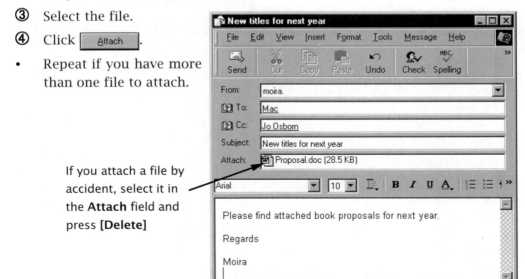

Receiving mail

To read a message that is in your Inbox:

- Double-click on a message to open it.
- If the preview pane is displayed, you can read the message in it rather than double-click to open a separate window.

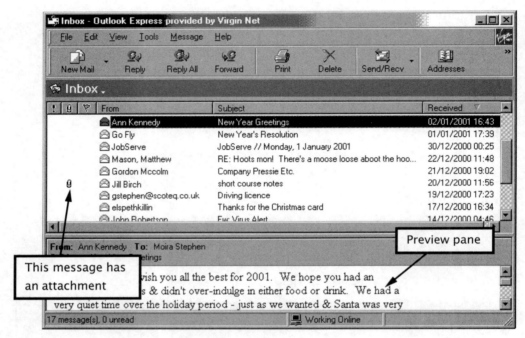

Reading an attachment

Beware of e-mail attachments – they are a common way of spreading viruses. Don't open attachments from unknown sources – and install anti-virus software on your PC

If a message has an attachment, a paperclip icon will be displayed beside it. If you use the preview pane, a paperclip is on the right of the header when the message is selected.

When you open the message, the name of the attachment will be displayed in the Attach field. There will be an icon beside it to indicate what application it was created in, e.g. Word.

- Double-click on the attachment name to open it.

The attachment will be opened in the application required to display it (provided that the application is on the PC).

Try it: Save an attachment

① Open the message (double-click on it).

② Open the **File** menu.

③ Choose **Save Attachments**...

④ Select the attachment(s) you wish to save.

⑤ Locate the folder you wish to save them in.

⑥ Click **Save**.

Reply

Messages may be replied to – just to the sender or to all on the original distribution list – or forwarded to another address.

Try it: Reply to or forward a message

① Select the message in your Inbox – click on it.

② Click the ![Reply] , ![Reply All] or ![Forward] tool (depending on what you wish to do).

If you are replying to a message you may or may not want to include the original message in your reply. You can switch the **Include message in reply** option on/off as required.

From the Inbox, open the **Tools** menu, choose **Options**, and then select the **Send** tab. Under the **Sending** heading, select or deselect the Include message in reply checkbox as necessary and click **OK**.

③ If you are forwarding the message, enter the address or addresses in the **To: Cc:** and **Bcc:** fields as necessary.

④ Complete the message (in same way as you would a new message).

⑤ Click **Send**.

11
Buying a PC

IN THIS CHAPTER:

- Working out what you need
- Your budget
- Where to buy one
- Buyers' checklist

Buying a PC may seem a bit daunting to the uninitiated, but it isn't as complicated as it may sound at first. This chapter contains a few tips to get you started. It's a bit like buying a new audio system, washing machine or car – you have to work out a balance between what you need, what you would like, and what you can actually afford! Do some homework first, weigh up the options, speak to friends and colleagues, decide what you want, and then go for it!

What do you need?

Before you go out and buy a computer you should do some research first. Try and work out:

- What you want your computer to be able to do now

- What you think you will want to be able to do with it in the future (by future I suggest you consider the next two or three years – any longer and you'll probably be thinking about updating your machine!)

Once you have some idea of your immediate and future requirements, you are on the way to working out the *specification* of computer you will require.

The *specification* can vary considerably from one computer to another. Items to note include:

Processor type – you'll need a Pentium III or IV (or Celeron) if you intend to surf the Net and run new business software (e.g. Microsoft Office 2000), or a fast Pentium IV or AMD (500 MHz or above) for a good gaming machine.

Amount of memory (RAM) – the very minimum you should go for is 32Mb, but 64Mb would be better in most situations. If you think that you'll use your PC for surfing the net, or run several applications at the same time, or play the new games (perhaps some across the Internet) you might want to consider going up to 128Mb of RAM.

Hard disk size – the bigger the better. If you're using it for home accounts and word processing you could go as low as 4Gb, but if you're into the powerful games don't go below 10Gb.

Monitor size – 14" and 15" are the cheapest, but 17" are now quite affordable and are more comfortable to use even if all you do is word processing (they tend to be standard if you get a better PC). You might want to consider splashing out on a 19" or 21" monitor if you're into games.

Speed of the modem (if it has one) – if you think you'll be on the Internet a lot, a faster modem will help keep your phone bills down.

Whether it has a CD and/or DVD drive – nearly all new software is supplied on CD-ROM so you'll need a CD drive to install software. If you want to be able to record onto CDs you'll need a drive that allows this too. If you want to watch DVD videos, you'll need a DVD drive. DVD drives can read CDs, but CD drives can't read DVD disks.

Video card – if you're intending to watch MPEG-2 (a file format used by some videos) encoded DVD-ROM movies at full speed, or play games that have 3-D graphics, a video card with 4 or 8Mb of SGRAM will allow you to do so.

How much will I spend?

No matter what you buy, it is often a compromise between what you would really like and what you can afford (or what you are prepared to spend on the item).

The higher the specification of computer, the more expensive it is. A machine with a fast processor, a lot of RAM, a big hard disk and 21" monitor will cost a lot more than a more modest system. As a rough guide, you could spend anything from about £400 to £2500 on a new PC.

If your budget is £500 you're unlikely to get a fast Pentium III with 128Mb of RAM, 21" monitor and 20Gb hard drive, but if all you're going to do is some word processing and basic spreadsheet work you don't *need* a fast Pentium III with 128Mb of RAM, 21" monitor and 20Gb hard drive!

Once you've worked out what you want from your computer, and how much you can afford to spend on it, you can start looking for the best specification of machine that is within your budget. If you can afford it, look for a machine that will suit your immediate and future needs.

Horses for courses

The examples below give a general guide to the type of specifications required for different areas of work.

If you want a computer for word processing, e.g. letters, reports, a book, etc. and perhaps help you keep your home accounts in order, you don't need a PC with a particularly

You can get assistance on working out PC specifications at www.iwantanewpc .co.uk

The site also gives advice on where to purchase your computer, and what price you would expect to pay! Worth a visit!

high specification. A second-hand one might do the trick! The following specification would probably suffice:

- Intel 486 (or similar) chip or higher

- 32 or 64Mb of RAM

- 4Gb hard disk (minimum)

- 15" monitor

If you want a computer to play the new interactive 3-D games on, or games across the Internet, you'd need:

- A fast Pentium III – 500 MHz or above (or an AMD K6, or an AMD Athlon)

- 64 or 128Mb of RAM

- 10Gb hard disk

- 17", 19" or 21" monitor

If you want to surf the Net as well as run standard business/home software, you could consider a:

- Pentium II or III processor (or an AMD K6)

- Between 32 and 128Mb of RAM

- 6Gb (minimum) hard disk

- 15", 17" or 19" monitor

Another factor to consider is how much you will be able to upgrade your computer in the future. You may well find that in 12 to 24 months, it is still working fine, but you could do with more disk space, or more memory. You might want to add a DVD drive or a digital camera or scanner (if they weren't part of the original purchase), so you should ask your supplier how many spare slots there are in the machine and whether or not you could add extra peripherals in the future.

Where should I buy a computer?

Mail order, e.g. Dell, Gateway

Look in any PC magazine for details. The machine will be delivered and you'll have to unpack the boxes and plug the machine together.

Possible disadvantages:

- You can't see it in action before ordering it.

- If anything is wrong (or is missing when you unpack the boxes or doesn't work when you plug it together) you can't just nip to your local shop to get it sorted out.

High street retailer or superstore, e.g. Dixons, PC World

These companies supply PCs suitable for home use. They usually have a good selection of hardware and software in store so you can see what you're getting before you buy it.

Local computer shop

The prices might not be as good as those in a PC superstore, and the range of machines available may be more limited. However, if you've a good local supplier upgrades and maintenance may be easier for you.

Internet

Be careful that you choose a reputable supplier - steer clear of anything that seems remotely dodgy! You could try **http://www.evesham.co.uk**

Second-hand computer shop

If you're after a basic PC to run some word processing and spreadsheet software you might find something suitable (and very reasonably priced) in a shop that sells second hand PCs.

However, if you are going to have to buy new software to install on the machine you may find that the new software doesn't run satisfactorily (or at all) on the second hand PC. For example, to run Microsoft Office 2000 you'll need a Pentium 75MHz (minimum), Windows 95, 98, NT or 2000, 32Mb of RAM, about 140Mb disk space and a CD-ROM (the software isn't supplied on diskette).

Upgrading an older computer can end up being a thankless and costly task, so if you are thinking of buying an older machine to upgrade, forget it – you'll nearly always find it cheaper in the long run to pay more initially and go for a new (or newer) machine.

Speak to friends or colleagues who have bought a PC recently. Find out who supplied them and what they thought of the service. Find out if their machine is reliable, and how helpful the suppliers are, etc.

Local paper

You may pick up a bargain. Perhaps someone has bought a new PC, and then decided to sell it (they may have upgraded). Make sure that you see it working, and get the purchase receipt and warranty details if at all possible.

Buyers' checklist

If you are buying a new PC, it can be useful to draw up a 'buyers' checklist', so you don't forget to ask anything you consider important. In particular, find out about:

Delivery time

Check that this is acceptable before you place your order.

Warranty options

Your statutory rights mean that the goods must be fit for the purpose for which they are sold. If you buy a PC that doesn't work you can get a full replacement or refund. You also have manufacturers' warranties, normally for 12 months (though some, e.g. Dell, now do three years) covering each item.

Optional extended warranties, e.g. up to three years, are offered by most suppliers.

Delivered systems

Check that all the cables, etc. are there before you start to plug your system together. If anything has been damaged in transit or is missing, call the supplier and arrange for the parts to be provided, or damaged goods to be replaced.

Some retailers will deliver your machine, plug it together and make sure that it is working properly before they leave

Faulty machines

If your PC doesn't work when you plug it together, contact your supplier. You may be expected to return the system to base (back to the supplier) or the supplier may arrange for the collection of the machine. They may or may not offer a replacement machine (they might try to fix the problem first).

Keep the boxes your PC came in just in case anything goes wrong – you'll need them if you have to return it.

12
Glossary

Access time: the time taken for the unit to search for, identify and process data saved on the disk – measured in milliseconds (msec) for a HDD.

Active window: the window that you are working in.

Address: the name given to a cell on a worksheet, e.g. B7, D22.

Address Book: similar to ordinary address book. An area for recording and updating contact details.

Application software: software that performs a specific task e.g. word processing, spreadsheet, desktop publishing.

ATM: Automatic teller machine.

Back-up: a procedure where files are copied for security reasons.

BIT: Binary Digit – 0 or 1.

Browser: software that allows you to surf the Net, e.g. Internet Explorer or Netscape Navigator.

Byte: 8 bits (0s and 1s). Each character, e.g. a, z, !, 5, etc. takes up 1 byte of storage.

CD-R: Compact Disk – Recordable. You can record onto this type of CD once.

CD-ROM: Compact Disk – Read Only Memory. Usually used to distribute computer applications – you can read what's on them but can't record onto them.

CD-RW: Compact Disk – Re-Writable. You can record and re-record onto this type of CD.

Central Processing Unit (CPU): the brains of your computer – where your text and data is sorted, calculated and manipulated as required.

Clock speed: the speed at which a CPU can process data.

Computer Aided Design/Computer Aided Manufacturing (CAD/CAM): applications used to design components on screen. The same software then uses the design information to control the machine that manufactures the component.

Database: an application package for storing and manipulating records, e.g. customer records, supplier information, product information, personnel records.

Desktop: the work area displayed when you start Windows.

Desktop publishing: application package that will produce newsletters, leaflets, etc.

Dialog box: an area where you can select and set options.

Digital Versatile Disk (DVD): disks with a storage capacity of 4–5 Mb. They can store video, text, graphics, audio, etc.

Disk: the main storage device on a PC.

Diskettes: a removable storage device.

Document: name given to a Word file.

Drives: a device that houses a disk – there are hard drives, diskette drives, Zip drives, CD drives, etc.

E-commerce: a rapidly expanding business area where organisations sell their products over the Internet.

Electronic Data Interchange (EDI). Allows many operations in business to be fully automated – stock control, re-ordering, invoicing, despatch and payment.

E-mail: Electronic mail – messages that can be sent over a network or the Internet. Messages can be sent, received, replied to, forwarded, etc.

Extension: Three characters at the end of file name that identify the application type.

Field: a piece of data within a record in a database table, e.g. Firstname, Surname, DOB, etc..

Filter: a feature used in database applications to extract records that meet specific criteria from your table(s).

Fixed disk: not removable – your local fixed disk is probably in your C: drive. You may have access to others over a local area network.

Floppy disk: another name for a diskette.

Folder: an area on a disk used to hold data and application files. You can create folders to help you organise your data files. Other folders are set up on your computer when you install software.

Footer: area at bottom of page for text, page numbers, filename, etc. that you want to have repeated on each page.

Frame: A container that objects may be placed within on a page – usually used in desktop publishing packages.

Gigabyte (Gb): 1024 megabytes.

Handouts: usually produced in presentation packages, e.g. PowerPoint. They consist of smaller versions of your slides that can be printed several to a page.

Hard copy: a term used for printouts.

Hard disk: non-removable storage device for programs and data.

Hardware: the physical parts of a computer. Input, processing, output and storage devices are all items of hardware.

Header: area at top of page for text, page numbers, filename, etc. that you want repeated on each page.

Hertz: cycles per second.

Home page: The term given to the page that appears on your screen when you open your browser application. You can specify the page that you wish to be your home page.

Hyperlink: A hyperlink is a 'hot spot' that lets you jump from one place on a page to another place on the same page or from one page to another, or to a different Web site altogether.

Icon: picture that represents an object or command.

Inactive window: one that is open, but not the one that you are working in.

Inbox: the area of your e-mail application where messages you receive are placed.

Indent: space between the margin and text/picture.

Information and Communication Technology (ICT): encompasses facsimile, telephone, multimedia presentations, etc. as well as computers.

Information management software: electronic organisers, e.g. electronic diaries.

Information society: a society where an increased proportion of the population works with and has access to vast amounts of information via the Internet.

Information technology (IT): a term that refers to any means of storing, processing and transmitting information using modern technology (computers).

Input device: any device that enables you to enter data or give instructions to your computer, e.g. keyboard or mouse.

Insertion point: black, flashing, vertical bar. Indicates where text or data will appear on the screen when you type.

Integrated Services Digital Network (ISDN). A newer, quicker, more reliable network than the PSDN, that transmits data in digital, not analogue, form..

Internet: not a single network, but a collection of thousands of computer networks worldwide.

Internet service provider (ISP): a company that provides access to the Internet.

Justification: the alignment of text/data on a page, within cells, etc.

Kerning: Also known as 'letter kerning', is the adjustment of space between certain pairs of letters in a word.

Keyboard: an input device.

Keyboard shortcuts: alternative method (instead of using menus or toolbars) of giving instructions.

Kilobyte (Kb): 1024 bytes.

Laptop: a small portable PC.

Leading: the amount of spacing between lines of text.

Local Area Network (LAN): computers linked together in a local area to facilitate sharing peripherals and data.

Margin: space between the edge of the paper and text/pictures.

Maximise: fill the screen.

Mega: million.

Megabyte (Mb): 1024 kilobytes.

Microprocessor: a CPU constructed on a single chip.

Minimise: reduce the window to a button on the Taskbar.

Modem: Modulator/Demodulator. A device that allows the PC to connect to the telephone system and use e-mail and the Internet. It changes (modulates) the digital signal used by computers into an analogue wave for transmission over the telephone line, and changes incoming signals to digital.

Mouse: an input device.

Multimedia system: a computer that can run application software, play music, playback video, run games software, access the Internet, etc.

Network: computers linked together so that they can share resources and transfer information.

Object: the generic name given to a block of text, a picture, WordArt, table, graph, etc. in a file.

Office Assistant: animated character that fronts the online help in Microsoft Office.

On-line Help: Help pages available on your computer.

Operator: the +, -, *, /, >, <, >=, <= etc. used in formulas.

Orientation: direction the paper is in – portrait (tall) or landscape (wide).

Operating System (OS): software that the computer needs to function, e.g. Windows 98, Me or 2000.

Outbox: the area of your e-mail application where messages you have ready to send are placed.

Output device: any device that allows what is on your PC to be seen or heard, e.g. printer, VDU, speakers.

Peripheral: any piece of equipment attached to a PC, e.g. keyboard, printer, speakers, rather than built into it.

Personal Computer (PC): a desktop computer, designed for individual use.

Pixels: dots of light on the screen.

Power On Self Test (POST): a series of tests that a computer runs automatically when it starts.

Presentation: an application package that produces slides and documentation for meetings, lectures, conferences.

Primary Key: the field(s) that uniquely identifies a record in a database table.

Printer: an output device used to produce printouts (hard copy) of your files.

Public Switched Data Network (PSDN). The telephone network that most of us are connected to from our homes, and that uses analogue rather than digital transmission.

Query: extracts, sorts or performs calculations on data in a database.

Random Access Memory (RAM): volatile memory – when the computer is switched off anything in RAM is lost.

Record: a record contains information about a single item in a database table.

Recycle Bin: folder in which deleted items are placed.

Refresh rate (or scan rate): the frequency at which the dots of light flash on the screen. Typically, 60 times per second.

Removable disk: one that you can remove from your PC, e.g. a diskette, CD, DVD, Zip disk.

Resolution: the number of pixels on the screen. Generally speaking, the more pixels the better the picture. A resolution of 640 × 480 means that there are 640 pixels across, 480 down the screen. A resolution of 800 × 600 is also common.

Restore: return a window to its previous size.

Read Only Memory (ROM): you can read from it but can't write to it.

Search engine: a system that keeps a database of what's on Web pages and in sites so that you can search for the information that you're interested in.

Secondary storage: devices on which you can store your work, e.g. disks, CDs, DVDs, etc.

Sent Items: the area of your e-mail application in which messages you have sent are placed.

Shortcut menu: restricted menu giving options that are most regularly used.

Slide: the individual pages in a presentation.

Software: the programs that make your computer work. The operating system (OS), e.g. Windows, and your applications e.g. Word, Works or Publisher.

SoHo: small office/home office. A term often associated with home working.

Spreadsheet: an application package that can perform calculations and produce graphs. Used for budgets, sales figures and anything involving calculations.

Startup disk: a disk that can be used to start your system if you have problems starting Windows.

Supercomputer: a very powerful mainframe.

Surfing: jumping from one location to another following hyperlinks of interest on the Internet.

Table: layout device for positioning text and data in rows and columns. In a database, the object in which data is stored.

Template: the pattern on which a file is based. It determines the page size, font styles, colour scheme, etc.

Toggles: switches on and off.

Toolbar: row of buttons (tools) giving shortcuts to commands.

Trackball: an input device, similar to an upside-down mouse.

Tracking: Also known as 'track kerning', this is the adjustment of spacing between all characters.

Transition: A special effect that can be used between slides in a slide show.

Uniform Resource Locator (URL): the address of a Web page or site.

Video conferencing: a facility that allows business meetings to take place between people in different locations (towns or even countries) without them having to spend time and money travelling.

Virus: a piece of software that has been written with the specific purpose of causing havoc on computer systems.

Visual Display Unit (VDU): the computer screen or monitor.

Wide Area Network (WAN): network that connects computers that are geographically remote, e.g. in different towns/countries/continents.

Wizard: a helpful tool for creating new objects when working in an application. Wizards are often used to help you set up a table in a database, or create a desktop publishing file.

Word processor: an application package that can be used to produce letters, reports, minutes, memos, etc.

Workbook: name given to an Excel file.

Index